MANAGE LIKE YOU OWN IT

MANAGE LIKE YOU OWN IT

MACK HANAN

amacom

American Management Association

New York • Atlanta • Boston • Chicago • Kansas City • San Francisco • Washington, D.C.
Brussels • Mexico City • Tokyo • Toronto

This book is available at a special
discount when ordered in bulk quantities.
For information, contact Special Sales Department,
AMACOM, a division of American Management Association,
135 West 50th Street, New York, NY 10020.

This publication is designed to provide accurate and authoritative
information in regard to the subject matter covered. It is sold
with the understanding that the publisher is not engaged in
rendering legal, accounting, or other professional service. If legal
advice or other expert assistance is required, the services of a
competent professional person should be sought.

Library of Congress Cataloging-in-Publication Data

Hanan, Mack.
    Manage like you own it / Mack Hanan.
        p. cm.
    Includes index.
    ISBN 0-8144-5112-8
    1. Industrial management.   I. Title.
HD31.H31243   1994
    658—dc20   93-44274
                                                                  CIP

Printing number

10 9 8 7 6 5 4 3 2 1

To
Bill Gerow,
who overcame
being "a good engineer"
to become a grower of
his business, his customers, and me

Contents

Preface: Monday Morning Action

On the first Monday of each month, twelve months a year, the chairman gathers together the company's top managers for what he calls his Monday Morning Action. It is a command performance. Only death would be considered an acceptable excuse. Even then, it would have to be authenticated.

After the confessional during which the chairman's managers compare where their businesses are to where they often regret they have said they planned them to be, the highlight of the meetings is the Question of the Month. The chairman always writes it out in his finely wrought, cursive penmanship on a small piece of white paper that he folds over exactly twice and tucks away in the upper left-hand pocket of his vest—over the place where, as someone once said, his heart would normally have been.

This month, he announces that the question is "a real doozie." "What," he asks, "is our company's single greatest resource?" As soon as he reads it, he looks up as he always does, at the manager he has chosen to lead off the discussion. There is no time to think. The chairman wants top-of-the-head answers because they are the only kind he trusts. Thinking only dilutes first impressions, he believes, and first impressions, he also believes, are the only true revelations of a manager's knowledge. Thinking, in the chairman's terms, is an attempt to deceive.

"Our R&D is our single greatest resource," the first manager answers. "It gives us our innovative edge. Nobody can design and develop new products faster and get them to

market first as consistently as we do. Our development people are number one. They get my vote."

The chairman writes it down.

"Not to gainsay R&D," the next manager answers—he
knows he is next because the answers always proceed clock-
wise from the first manager who is called on—"but what good
is product development without the manufacturing capacity
to standardize new products at high levels of quality for mass
production as the low-cost supplier? That's what our manufacturing people do. I'd say that they are our single greatest
resource."

The chairman writes it down.

The third manager nominates marketing. The fourth manager extolls the information-technology people who maintain
the nervous system of the business. And so it goes around the
room—another manager, another resource—and the chairman
writes it all down. Close to the end, it comes the turn of a
manager who enjoys an independent income.

"If everyone who has spoken is correct, then no one is
correct," he says. "There can only be one single greatest
resource. The reason no one has mentioned it so far is that no
one manages it. The reason that no one manages it is because
it exists outside our company, beyond our control. Yet without
it, none of us would be here to give our self-serving answers.
Our single greatest resource is our *customers*."

No one says anything as the chairman writes it down.
The manager goes on. "Our customers are the source of our
business," the manager says. "Without them, who would our
R&D design and develop products for? Who would we standardize manufacturing for? Who would we market to? Who
would pay us? Our customers are not just the source of our
business. They are the source of our funds. They are our
company's single greatest resource."

Finally, the chairman speaks. "If that is the answer, what
do I need all of *you* for? What do all of you need *me* for?"

"For the same reason," the manager with the independent income sums up. "To create added value for our single
greatest resource. That way, it can become an even greater
resource—and make us even greater along with it."

MANAGE LIKE YOU OWN IT

Introduction: Focus

"The operative word is *focus*."

After a roller-coaster business history of ups and downs from being underpriced, overcosted, and, along with competitors National Semiconductor and Advanced Micro Devices, more dependent on being protected by Uncle Sam than being valued by customers, Intel CEO Andrew Grove has come to the conclusion that you have to put all your effort behind the one thing that you do best and then not hedge your bets. If you hedge, you're much more likely to lose. Even if you win, you win only in a mediocre way. If you focus and you're right, you win big time.

Focus has become today's management mantra. It did not just come out of nowhere; focus has always been around. But the main thing that is different today is what you must focus *on*.

It may not be what you think. Nor is it what most managers have thought for all the years up to now.

In every industry, two major competitors are coming to dominate the business. Number three, if there still is one, is on borrowed time. Each winner is a "competitive company"—a line of business that has rededicated its mission to be a provider of competitive advantages to its customers instead of just a supplier of products and services.

Competitors 1, 2, and 3 in each industry are far more similar than different. The distinctive difference between them is their managers. The manager who operates best as an "owner" has the best chance to be number one: to run the most competitive company.

Regardless of what you manage—products or services for

consumer, industrial, or technical markets—your focus must be on improving the *outcomes* of the customer operations you affect. Your first thought on being given a franchise to "manage like you own it" must not be, "How can I make money with this business?" but rather "Who else's business can I help make money with *my* business?"

If a customer operation is a contributor of a certain amount of cost before you lay hands on it by intervening with your products or services, it must make a lesser contribution when you take your hands away. If a customer line of business contributes a certain amount to revenues, it must make a greater contribution or make its contribution faster or less expensively after you have touched it. Either way or both ways, you must make sure that it contributes more to customer profitability because of you.

Customer outcomes have to be the focal point of your business vision. They are a customer's net realized values from doing business with you. Continuously improving them has to be your business mission. Now that almost all products and services have become commodities, your ability to make customers more competitive by making them lower-cost producers or more-profitable marketers is your sole remaining differentiator. It is why customers will choose to do business with you: not because you have unique capabilities or your products have proprietary specifications, but because you are able to manage exceptional results from applying them to your customers' assets.

Outcomes are the results your customer gets from making whatever he makes or serving whomever he serves. Outcomes are your customer's bread and butter. Improving them is yours. In order to become an improver of customer businesses, you must raise the sights of your vision. Managing your own assets cost-effectively is no longer enough. First and foremost, you must be the preferred co-manager of your customers' assets as well.

How good a co-manager you are determines your competitiveness. Without co-management skills, you lack the capability to be a candidate for major customer partnerships. Customers may *compliment* you for the excellence of your assets. They benchmark high on the scale of "best practices." But unless you can *complement* the management of their own assets to improve their outcomes, your capabilities remain unanswered costs and your resources will stay in inventory.

What is the business of your customers? Your answer will tell you what your own business must be:

- If your customers are in packaged-goods supermarketing, your business must improve their revenue outcomes by turning over each square foot of shelf space their products occupy faster and at higher margins or lower cost.
- If your customers are in manufacturing, your business must improve their revenue outcomes by increasing the productivity of each dollar's worth of labor, materials, and energy, or improve their cost outcomes by reducing inventory, downtime, and scrap.
- If your customers are in health care, your business must improve their patient outcomes by faster and more accurate diagnosis, disease-specific treatment, and timely discharge.

Keying In on the Three Kingdoms

Focus on customer outcomes would be good doctrine at any time. It has become essential doctrine for the 1990s as corporate lines of business are being made increasingly autonomous and their managers are empowered to manage each business "like they own it."

In the 1990s, you will succeed insofar as you can make the switch from managing in the old corporate tradition of being somewhat good at many things to becoming very good at a few things. These few things will be your keys to getting on top of your business and then getting your business to the top of its industry. On the way up, you will pass the managers who have become soft and paunchy with the well-roundedness that became fashionable—and was survivable—in the 1980s.

By fixating on improving customer outcomes, you can focus on two types of ownership requirements for your core personal capabilities:

First, you must own "the vision" in your industry—the foresight to see, better than your competitors, the most cost-effective business strategy that allows you to apply your technology, whatever it may be, to a market to improve its outcomes.

Second, you must become a crusader for your vision. With it, you can seize three kingdoms:

1. *The Kingdom of Applications.* To be the Applications King, you must own the people who are the best customizers of your technology to each customer's human and physical assets. Without customization, you will be a commodity business. With a commodity business, you die a slow-but-sure marginless death. To avoid commoditization, your people must have the sharpest applications skills, foremost among which are consultation, information, education, implementation, and evaluation of their results. Consulting must not simply be a service they sell. Total Consultative Management (TCM) must be the umbrella discipline over everything they do to improve customer outcomes.

2. *The Kingdom of Margins.* To be the Margin King, you must own your industry's standards for continuously improving customer outcomes so that you merit superior margins as your share of their gain. This will enable you to brand your contributions.

3. *The Kingdom of Productivity.* To be the Productivity King, you must own the most-integrated work flows. You must operate them at the fastest cycle times to maximize the rate at which you can turn over the values you add to customer outcomes. In this way, your improvement of customer competitiveness can be continuous.

What about quality? Why is there no Kingdom of Quality for you to own? You cannot own quality. Your customers own it. They set its standards, not you. They define it in their own terms, measure it with their own yardsticks, and set the lower limits beneath which they will not buy and the upper limits above which they will not pay a premium. This is what their "good enough" range of fulfillment is all about: good enough quality for customer satisfaction.

Applications are your key to margins. The only things you can get paid high margins for are the results of putting your products and services to work in a customer's operations and making a positive difference in their contribution to profits. Your profits will be a derivative of your customer's profits. The before-and-after difference in the customer's results—not any difference in your products and services—are the only viable basis for margins. Alone among your capabilities, applications skills drive these differences.

Margins are your key to profits. Under 1990s rules, where markets are not just niched but microniched, you can no longer "make it up on volume" if you give your margins away. Discounted prices give away the keys to the kingdom. Discounted prices multiplied by volume give away the kingdom.

Productivity is your key to profit continuity. You must get your applications into your markets first, get them out fast, and keep them coming on an uninterrupted basis to deny competitive entry. The more productively you generate your applications, the more of a track record you can accumulate as an improver of customer outcomes. Your track record is the sole creditable support of your claim to be the industry standard of value to customer outcomes.

Focusing on the three kingdoms demands concentration. Most managers suffer from diffusion. Everything gets a love tap, but few things get punched home. In order to find a role model for concentrating on the essentials in the world of the 1990s, you have to look outside the Fortune 500 corporate frame of reference to owner-managers, the "little guys" that corporate managers are always warned to watch out for because they have something that corporate managers do not: focus.

Owner-managers have traditionally been held in a mix of scorn and envy by corporate managers. They are scorned for their undercapitalized asset bases, their hole-in-the-wall facilities, and the humdrum names ("Pep Boys"; "Manny, Moe, and Jack") that personalize them to their markets. They are envied for their ability to niche the hearts out of corporate markets and keep their management teams together year after year so that they get to be very good at what they focus on doing.

One thing that the little guys get to be very good at is being their customers' co-managers. Because they set themselves up to be line extensions of their customers' businesses—in a very real sense, as if they were once part of a customer's internal operations that have been outsourced but still remain responsible for contributing to the outcomes they affect. They work up close, like insiders, breathing down each customer's neck, and looking over his or her shoulders, so they can focus on outcomes. Their customers' stake is their own. They take a share of them to the bank. Little guys learn from day one where their profits come from—not from their own products or services but from their shares of the customer outcomes they improve. They never let that essential truth out of their sight.

Managing a corporate business "like you own it" is managing as an owner-manager. It is very different from managing like someone else owns it. As long as a business is someone else's, it can remain unfocused: Its last dollar of cost can remain uncontrolled, its last dollar of revenue can be left on the table, its last unit of productivity can be left on the conference room floor or in the factory scrap bin, and the result of its last cycle of innovation can be left on the market one day longer than it is able to sustain its margins.

Roberto Goizueta, chairman of Coca-Cola Co., has a formula for a manager that is every bit as valuable as the formula for Coke: someone who can keep costs in line while achieving sales and earnings growth and enhanced shareholder value. Anything less than that is unworkable. Anything more is gravy.

Becoming "That Guy"

The power to manage a company's lines of business like an owner-manager is coming down. Once concentrated entirely at the top, power is increasingly being distributed to managers of profit-centered strategic business units (SBUs) to operate autonomously, make joint ventures, outsource capabilities, and partner with suppliers. Chief Operating Officers are becoming vestigial. Middle managers are increasingly acting as their own chief operators.

ALCOA is an example of distributed power as shown in the high-autonomy organization model in Figure I-1. One of Paul O'Neill's first acts as chairman was to change "the flow of power from the traditional path in corporations to give business unit leaders the responsibility to be the quarterbacks." This means they are free to call their own plays. They can source their businesses internally or go outside, sell products and services whether they make them or not, and run a business composed only of intellectual assets and a line of credit. Instead of looking to the chairman for leadership, they can focus on leading their markets. Not only does the CEO

Figure I-1. High-autonomy organization model.

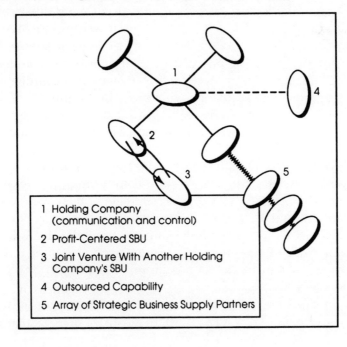

1 Holding Company
  (communication and control)

2 Profit-Centered SBU

3 Joint Venture With Another Holding
  Company's SBU

4 Outsourced Capability

5 Array of Strategic Business Supply Partners

not intervene in their operations; no one intervenes between them and their CEO.

General Motors has organized its Saturn Corporation as if it were a "virtual corporation" made up of small focused business units. Each self-directed team manages its own unit's budget without direct oversight from top management. The team hires and fires on its own, controls its inventory, and manages innovation.

Saturnization is gradually taking place in the traditional divisions of General Motors, where the monolithic concept of running a business is on the way out. The old, top-down corporate culture is giving way to a new, no-excuses style of doing business. General Motors is vesting ownership of each model line in a single manager, who is colloquially referred to as "that guy" and who has bumper-to-bumper, road-to-roof authority. He is empowered with his own financial resources, manufacturing and diemaking capability, and product engineers —everything he needs to produce a world-class vehicle. As a result, there are no excuses for missing his targets on cost, weight, or fuel economy, or for missing performance goals. Nor is there any excuse for missing out on customer satisfaction.

One-stop ownership has also come to service businesses. At Aetna Life & Casualty Insurance, a single manager has been put in charge of processing each claim that comes in, seeing it through from start to finish in place of almost the dozen agents and adjusters who used to be involved. The manager "owns" the claim, taking on a double role: Aetna's relationship manager with the customer and process manager of the claim.

GM's "guys" and the guys at Aetna are earning a name for themselves in the investment community, where their companies' stocks are traded. They are being called "cannibals" for the way that they use innovative strategies to gobble up past successes, no matter how glorious they may have been, in order to feed the future. Cannibals are characterized by their focus. According to cannibal lore, "Focus is synonymous with success."

Cannibals do not apologize for running small businesses. They agree with Bill Gates of Microsoft that "size dilutes the skillset of the founding people" and that growth contains a threat to the creativity of new developments. They know that their brainworkers and the vision that drives them are their core assets. Beyond that, they are comfortable owning little or nothing else because they can gain easy access inside and outside to whatever they need whenever they need it.

You can be a cannibal in a small company or in a large, diversified corporation as long as you keep on remaking your business before an upstart startup remakes it for you—but in his image, not yours. At Novell, a software maker, their cannibals try to be "two years ahead and gaining" in order to stay on the front edge of change.

Becoming "that guy" means being able to envision your business in a grandview manner while remembering to sweat the keyhole details that count toward your customers' outcomes. Knowing which details count is a critical success factor in managing "like you own it."

The president of Mazda Motor Corporation in Japan got there by learning what counts. Everyone in his North American operations remembers the day he called his transplant factory in Detroit to find out how they were attaching rearview mirrors. Were the holes being drilled properly? "What the hell kind of question is that for a president to be asking?" was the reaction of the American manager who took the call. As it turns out, the answer is *the right kind of question*.

Mazda's president was managing like he owned it, sweating a keyhole detail that has grandview implications for his business. He knows that rust can develop if the holes for the mirrors are not properly drilled. If rust develops, customer-satisfaction outcomes fall and sales outcomes fall with them. Even if only one sale were to be saved, it would pay for the phone call.

When you manage "like you do *not* own it"—when you have the traditional employee mindset of working *for* an owner instead of working *like one*—you risk undermanaging, overmanaging, or mismanaging your assets because they are not *your* assets. You risk becoming like the managers at B. F. Goodrich, Goodyear, and Firestone, who ignored the competitive innovation represented by radial tires. In the same way, you risk becoming like the managers at U.S. Steel and Bethlehem Steel, who ignored the innovative basic oxygen furnaces of foreign competitors because they had become managers by being successful with open hearths. You risk becoming like the managers at Allis-Chalmers, who could never focus on a workable model of costs, quality, and customer value that would make a profit. By 1989, the multimillion dollar Allis had shrunk to the revenues of a couple of top-level McDonald's stores.

When you add up all these examples, the only conclusion you can come to is that managing "like someone else owns it" has been pretty much the norm for American businesses, even in their so-called Golden Age from the 1960s to the 1980s. How else could businesses have gone on day after day with quality defects in one-third to two-thirds of a production run? With production per labor-hour one-half or less of what it could have been? With downtimes of 20 to 40 percent of total time? And with lead times and setup times often twice the length of an entire manufacturing cycle? Whoever owned these operations, it was not the managers who ran them.

Buying Into Owner's Assumptions

The decisions you make as a manager—whether you make Allis-type decisions or McDonald's-type—will be predetermined by your assumptions. Most of the "essential truths" of business that you have grown up with have lost their truthfulness, being just as flat as today's management hierarchies they still pretend to serve:

No-Longer Essential Truths

- No business remains small by choice.
- A business must be diverse so it can be countercyclical.
- Economies of mass are preferable to profits from specialization.
- Single-technology businesses are vulnerable.
- Product businesses are different from service businesses.

• Consumer and business-to-business businesses cannot learn anything of value from each other.

What assumptions will work for you in managing "like you own it?" Owners have their own sets of assumptions. If you buy into them for your own business, you will manage it in the belief that unnecessary costs are luxuries, including yourself. As a principal player, you are a principal cost.

You will also buy into the beliefs that margins are the proof that you—not your competitors—are managing your business; that your products and services are servants of their applications, since they cannot command high margins without being applied; that the relevance of your technology is dependent on how cost-effectively it can be applied to improve customer outcomes and not just to improve your own products or services; that product-and-service life cycles are shortening, market segments are subsegmenting, and major sources of supply are consolidating all around you while specialized suppliers are proliferating. Here is a checklist of ten owner's assumptions—the only ones that are safe to make in the 1990s. You should never leave home without them.

Owner's Assumptions

1. Your income is a function of your contribution to customer outcomes.
2. *Quality* is the zero-defect improvement of customer outcomes. *Productivity* is standardizing your ability to provide quality outcomes over and over again.
3. You cannot base your margins on your ownership of assets. You can only make margins by helping customers improve the way they manage their own assets.
4. Margins are the value that customers add to your business in return for the value of improved outcomes you add to their businesses.
5. Margin erosion can no longer be made up by added volume at low margins.
6. Your business growth depends on increasing the value of customer assets under your management while

minimizing the assets you must own to grow them.

7. Manage or be managed: Either manage the customer operations you sell into or a competitor will manage them—along with your margins.

8. A *brand* is a differentiated outcome. A *commodity* is an undifferentiated outcome at the level of an industry's average. Applications skills make brandable outcomes achievable with commodity products.

9. In a world of undifferentiated outcomes, only applications skills are bankable.

10. Superior outcomes are a momentary rate and not a permanent state.

No matter how it is presented to you, the English translation of your empowerment probably nets out something like this:

"We're handing you a proven business. This means that it is probably a commodity, essentially undifferentiated from your competitors'. Your technology is state-of-the-art, which means that it is also a commodity. Even if it were leading-edge, you would still have to apply it in ways that would make margins with it. But applications that are not customized quickly become commodities, too.

"While you are customizing your applications, their commercial life will be running out from underneath you. Competition will replicate every innovation you come up with and do it cheaper because they will learn all the hard parts from you. If you hang back and wait for them to go first, they may run away with one of your markets. Either way, whether you invest up-front or play catch-up, the pressure on your margins will be excruciating. It will get worse.

"Please don't take any of this personally. All your fellow managers enjoy similar working conditions. We are an equal-opportunity employer."

Under circumstances like these—which are not confined to the inner circle of Dante's Inferno but simply reflect today's global marketplace—how can you win?

To put it in one word: *Focus.*

Start each investment cycle with the customer outcomes

you want to improve as your objectives. Build the business team that can become their preferred provider. Run each business for margins so that volume can be the multiplier of margins rather than their substitute. Limit your assets to the point where your business would be profitable even in a no-growth economy. Create your strategies as if quality were equalized throughout your industry so that you can resist the temptation to differentiate your business by today's product or service performance ·specifications. Invest some of your savings from productivity in innovative scientific and marketing technology that can yield a continuous stream of new applications and the strategies to merchandise them. Run your business for short-term quantifiable results and the long term will take care of itself.

With customer outcomes as your objectives, you are able to "manage your business like you own it"—the same way Tom Watson ran the young IBM when he owned it. He owned margins that were up to two-thirds higher than his competitors. He owned applications. He may not have invented the strategy of managing a product-based business as if it were a service, but he became world-renowned for it. Companies that went head-to-head with him in the markets that he dominated always wondered how come Tom Watson got his margins. "We have comparable products," they would complain. "In many cases, our technology is superior. We give good service." But Tom Watson knew what they did not have. "If you want my margins," he would tell them, "you've got to have my philosophy."

Tom Watson's philosophy was marginally different. Like his competitors, he kept one hand in his customers' pockets. But with the other hand, he put more money in than he took out. This was his key to the three kingdoms.

Part One
Envisioning Ownership

1
Own the Vision

If you are going to manage your business "like you own it," you must have the most "needed" vision of a business in your industry—the vision that gives your customers the most compelling answer to the question, *What do I need you for?*

Nobody must be able to see a better way to bring continuous improvement to customer outcomes.

Unless you can envision a preemptive need for your business, it will not be preferred over the visions of competitive businesses. If it is not preferred, you will not make your margins.

Vision is not foreseeing the future. Vision is seeing your customers making the next cycle of incremental improvements to their competitiveness by applying your intellectual capital to the optimal product and service mix that implements its objectives. Why will it have to be *your* intellectual capital and *your* products and services in preference to someone else's? What do they need *you* for?

Test your foresight. Can you see your customers growing more competitive as a result of your applications skills and strategies? What kinds of competitive advantage do you see yourself helping them to gain? What outcomes do you see them achieving?

What capabilities do you see them requiring from you? What new or enhanced consultation, education, information, implementation, and evaluation skills do you see customers needing to add to their own? What values do you see them obtaining as a result? How do you see them measuring your added values? Which standards of improved customer performance do you see yourself having to meet if you are going to be their preferred value bringer?

What margins do you see your standards of performance justifying?

The "vision thing" is composed more of insight than foresight. The key to vision is how to see your customers using you as an agent of their continuous improvement. Do they use you to help control one of their cost-centered business functions? Do they use you to help expand one of their profit-centered lines of business? In either case, they are reaching out for you to empower them.

Vision is all about customer empowerment. What can your customers do with you that they cannot do without you? Can they grow bigger? Can they grow bigger faster? Can they grow bigger and faster more surely? You need a *yes* to at least two of these three questions. Otherwise, your customers cannot have the power to grow you in return. Without such a power exchange, there can be no partnering between you. Win-win is based on grow-grow.

Letting Customers Create Your Vision

Your business today represents past bets—yours, or the visionary gambles of your predecessors—about the future values your customers and clients would most likely find compelling. Each planning cycle that you go through represents your own next best bet. It is your chance to see eye-to-eye with your customers. Plans give you the opportunity to correct your vision for the farsightedness that can lead you to believe your customers will go on applying today's values far longer than they will. Plans also give you the opportunity to correct your vision for the nearsightedness that can lead you to enter markets too early with tomorrow's values.

How sharp is your vision?

Can you see how to make a continuing business out of word processing, where Wang, who owned the business, could not? Can you see how to make a continuing business out of workstations, where Apollo, who owned the business, could not? Can you see how to continue the success of businesses once owned by IBM, Sears, Kodak, and Westinghouse when they themselves could not? What makes your vision sharper than theirs?

The answer is *nothing*, unless you supplement your imperfect insight by letting your customers create your vision with you. This makes it market-ready from inception. It enables you to plug your business into their business from day one, as an adjunct power source with you as co-manager to each customer manager whose business you take on to grow.

Without customer insight, you cannot see the business for the products. Take a business that is built around a computerized product-design process. Its manager's temptation is to sell the features and benefits of the process compared to all other processes that can automate product design. Pricing is based on cost-plus, modified by prevailing competitive discount practices. Sometimes sales are made at cost-minus. The result is that margins get clobbered and jobs are sold just for their cash flow and just to keep bodies employed. Meanwhile, the applied values of the process never become known. If they were, each day a customer saves in time-to-market by accelerating the design cycle would be seen to pay over and over again for the process at full margins . . . and then some.

If a customer were to create your vision, he would go about it something like this:

> I am going to set you up in business. Your business has one overriding objective: to make my business more competitive. In order to ensure this, I am going to set you up as an outsource—as if you were one of my own internal business units that I have spun out and made autonomous. We will be two separate businesses with the same gene pool.
>
> Your job is to apply your products or processes or services or systems to improve my own products, processes, services, systems—to improve their productivity, their quality, their operating performance, their market acceptance, and their customer satisfaction.

As a result, the business functions of mine that you affect will become lower-cost contributors to my total costs of being a supplier. My lines of business that you affect will become higher-share marketers or higher-margin sellers.

If a customer were to create your vision this way, you would see your business in terms like these:

"I see my customer reordering.

"I hear him tell me why. His cash flows have improved by over a third since we helped him condense his order-entry-to-shipment cycle down to a single day for his biggest-winner products.

"I see him counting how many hundreds of thousands of dollars this adds to his business—a threefold multiple so far of what he has invested with us. I see him planning how he is going to put this new money to work to make other parts of his business more competitive.

"I see his people benefiting from larger bonuses as a result of their improved productivity and a customer satisfaction score that has practically doubled in the past six months.

"I see the customer inviting us to migrate our system across his other businesses where time-to-market is a critical success factor."

Keep your vision—and the process for envisioning it—simple. Reduce it to basics. Unless it is simple, you will tend to express it in a different way each time someone asks you what it is. You will have a hard time communicating it to your people. They will have a hard time understanding it. The result will be strategic dissonance. But even a simple vision that can be simply expressed is worthless unless it is *of* the customer, *by* the customer, and *for* the customer. This is why you have to let your customer write it for you.

Insisting on a No-Way-Out Vision

Visions are nonrefundable. There are virtually no returns or exchanges. Once you buy into a vision for your business, you own it. You can always change the words, but you cannot change your people and their applications skills without changing the very business itself. This is because your business is the expression of your people's applications skills. Your people must be "the people who..."—the people who own your industry's standard outcomes. Everything else is parsley, not steak.

Your vision must be concise and unambiguous. Unambiguity of vision leaves you with no way of fulfilling it. You must have no other gods than your vision, no fallbacks or backups. You must beware of contingent visions, even though you may think that they safeguard you by providing ways out. Quite the contrary, you will be tempted to adopt them at precisely the times when you most need to maintain your focus.

Take Seymour Cray as your model. His vision of his business, Cray Research, is to apply supercomputing technology to customers who need fast answers to complex product design and development questions that affect their time-to-market capabilities. Cray has no backup plans. He is not going into peripherals or services. Come what may, he is staying with "real supercomputers."

If you read into Cray's vision the doctrine of no excuses, you see a classic case of a manager's acceptance of the responsibility of business ownership.

No-way-out visions come from taking four successively narrower squints at your mission, as shown in Figure 1-1.

Squint number one: Focus on the minimal number of key customers in a key industry you serve whose growth you believe you can best drive over the next three to five years and whose growth, in turn, will drive your own.

Squint number two: Within each key customer's business, focus on the smallest number of critical success functions and lines of business to which you can make continuous improvements.

Figure 1-1.   Vision focal point.

AN INDUSTRY WHOSE GROWTH WE CAN DRIVE

A BUSINESS FUNCTION OR LINE OF BUSINESS
CRITICAL TO THIS INDUSTRY'S
COMPETITIVENESS THAT WE
CAN CONTINUOUSLY IMPROVE

A FACTOR CRITICAL TO THIS
FUNCTION'S OR BUSINESS LINE'S
COMPETITIVENESS THAT WE CAN
CONTINUOUSLY IMPROVE

THE SINGLE MOST COST-EFFECTIVE
APPLICATION OF OUR
CAPABILITY THAT CAN
DELIVER THE
IMPROVEMENT

Squint number three: Within each function and line of business, focus on the smallest number of critical success factors whose continuous improvement is necessary to enhance the contribution they make to their business function or line of business.

Squint number four: For each factor, focus on the single most cost-effective application with which you can deliver maximum added value. The added value will be your contribution to customer outcome—in other words, your *product*.

Arriving at Your Core Competencies

Your vision should be constructed backward, starting with the customers with whom it will end up:

1. What is a growing or growable market where I can make money by accelerating growth, or what is a dormant market where I can make money by regenerating growth?
2. What are the profit-centered lines of business and the cost-centered functions in such a market that are critical to its success?
3. What applications of which technical processes, products, and services can add sufficient, significant, predictable values to these lines of business and business functions so that the net outcomes merit premium margins?
4. What is the smallest number of core competencies I must own:

   • To provide the applied values.
   • To create the premium outcomes.
   • To merit the premium margins.
   • To do business with the smallest number of lines of business and business functions.
   • Within the smallest number of growing, growable, or regrowable customers.
   • In a market that is also growing, growable, or regrowable.

What you end up with is the smallest asset base for your business that you must be expert in. You will also know with whom you must apply your expertise in order to achieve outcomes that will allow you to value-base your margins. This process makes your vision real by equipping it with two attributes:

1. A price tag that will tell you its cost.
2. A basis in value that permits you to recover your price and make money on it.

You need to keep massaging your competencies until you can give the right customer-driven answers to two key questions:

- How small a number of competencies should make up my core? *Answer:* as few as necessary to deliver the added value of the outcomes I need to provide.
- How expert must my competencies be? *Answer:* as proficient as necessary to deliver the added value of the outcomes I need to provide.

Just when you think you have your capabilities properly structured, take another look at them through three assessments:

1. Does the business you envision make money for your customers by reducing their costs or increasing their revenues and earnings?
2. Does the business you envision make money for you? There are three criteria you have to assess:
   a. Is its *market potential* in terms of its most likely ability to generate a high share of available sales good enough to go ahead?
   b. Is its *realization potential* in terms of its most likely ability to generate high unit margins good enough to go ahead?
   c. Is its *capitalization potential* in terms of its most likely ability to generate sufficient, consistent, and pre-dictable cash flows that will make the business self-capitalizing good enough to go ahead?
3. Does the business you envision still go on making money for your customers and you when, as, and if your vision's exclusive ownership becomes shared by imitative competitors?

Testing Your Vision for Results

All visions look good in the dark, at the time you create them, when you cannot see a business as it will look, warts and all, over the next three to five years. Does your vision have "legs" so that your original investment can have many happy returns?

One of the most difficult tasks of owner-management is to

have to make this kind of prediction today about a result that will not make itself known until some time in the future. But unless you make it today, you can forget the future.

The profit/cost-effectiveness grid shown in Figure 1-2 can help you test your vision for results before you have to commit to it. The grid's horizontal axis measures the relative cost-effectiveness of a vision's position: how much of a bang you can expect to get in return for every buck you invest in making a business out of it. The grid's vertical axis measures the vision's most likely profit probability.

If you are starting a business from scratch, it will most likely be positioned near 1.0 on the horizontal axis of Figure 1-2 to acknowledge its high profit probability—otherwise, why get into it? Like all new businesses, it is likely to be low in cost-effectiveness until you learn how to run it lean and mean. By the time you do, it will have migrated to 4.5. In this space,

Figure 1-2. Profit/cost-effectiveness grid.

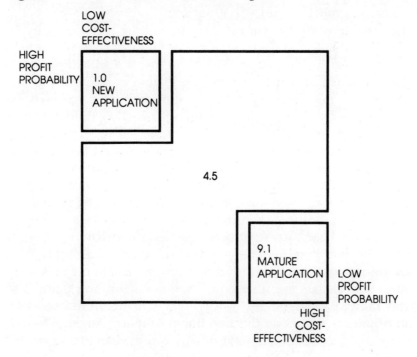

reminders come daily that managers get smart too slow and businesses get old too fast.

A 4.5 position on the grid says that you envision a medium-risk/medium-reward business. If you own it, you can look forward to enough cash flow to pay your bills and live on but little or no growth to reinvest. What you get out of managing a 4.5 business is only a little more than what you put in. Over time it progressively migrates to the 9.0 position on the grid as it matures. By that point, the outcomes from your applications have become commodities. When a business reaches 9.0 on the horizontal axis, you are finally managing it with ultimate cost-effectiveness. You have no choice. Anything less and you fall off the grid. But the tradeoff is unbearable pressure on margins. You will have squeezed out all the risk—except the risk that any day is the end game.

Envisioning a mature business in nontraditional ways can stretch its reward more than its risk. It requires "outsight," which is the power to see your business from outside itself: to see how you can extend its reach through "safe growth." If you run a railroad and you envision it traditionally, you see it as a transportation business. As you squint at it, you may be able to see it as a subsystem. The grandview vision into which it fits includes integrating the rail line with a truck line and a barge line. Integrating your freight system enables you to mix and match the three types of transportation to customize the most cost-effective distribution plan for each customer's shipping needs.

As Figure 1-3 shows, your original railroad becomes the hub of an enhanced overland and waterborne transport system. You have advanced your position up the value chain as a provider of improved customer outcomes. But your businesses are all commodities, mature businesses of the past.

If you use outsight and take another squint at your railroad, you may be able to visualize an enhanced definition of transportation: the movement of information. This may help you visualize a fiber-optic "rail line" running parallel to the railroad on its right-of-way that will distribute units of information alongside the traditional units of freight. Most of your cost base is already laid down. You have a "safe growth"

Figure 1-3. Safe growth.

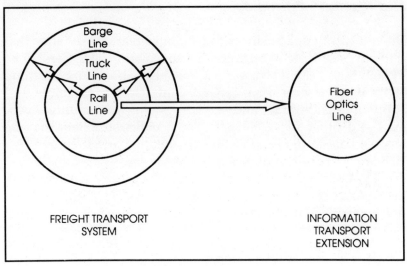

opportunity by simple extension, as Figure 1-3 shows. Because it is a high-growth business, your reward can significantly exceed your risk.

Visualizing Your Asset Base

As a provider of improved outcomes, you have a choice of three tiers of assets to lay down as the foundation for your business.

Tier one is composed solely of intellectual assets. It gives you a brainpower organization. Its core capabilities are delivery systems for applications expertise: consultation, education, information, implementation, and evaluation. If you need products or other services, you can obtain them from outside suppliers.

Tier two is composed solely of product and product-related service capabilities.

Tier three is a mix of types one and two.

Which model is the one for you?

Tiers One and Two: Pyramidless Peaks and Peakless Pyramids

Do you want your business to be a pure-play consultancy that can ally itself as a business partner with customers? The Pyramidless Peak, shown in Figure 1-4, manufactures nothing of its own. It acts as a general contractor to assemble and apply optimal product-and-service systems from multiple vendors and other consultancies. Some of its suppliers may be modeled along the lines of the technology partner shown as a Peakless Pyramid in Figure 1-5.

Pyramidless Peaks occupy Tier One. They are full business partners, allying themselves strategically with the business objectives of customers, linking themselves up to their

Figure 1-4. Pyramidless peak.

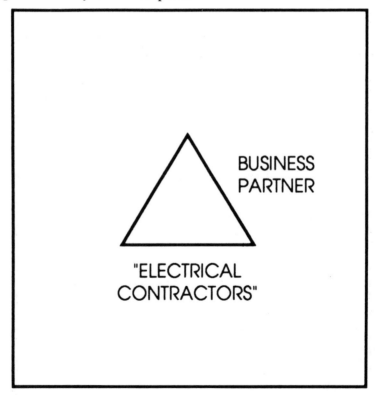

Figure 1-5. Peakless pyramid.

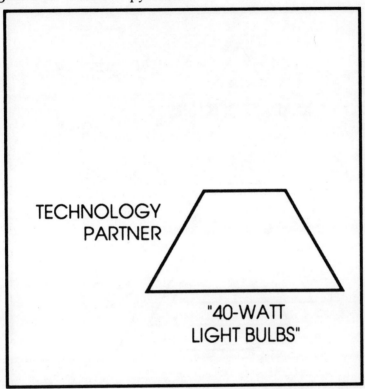

outcomes and acting as co-managers of the customer assets they affect. Peakless Pyramids, on the other hand, occupy Tier Two. They are manufacturers and vendors. They sell products on price and performance: they are the "feature and benefit" sellers of "forty-watt light bulbs" to "electrical contractors" who apply them in the Pyramidless Peaks. Their relationship is nicely symbiotic. But the margins are all with the Pyramidless Peaks because they are at the end of the value chain that touches the customer, lays hands on customer operations, and shares in the improved outcomes.

Tier Three: The Enterprise Model

Do you want your business to be a full-scale supplier of both products and applications consultation, with multivendor ac-

Figure 1-6.   Enterprise.

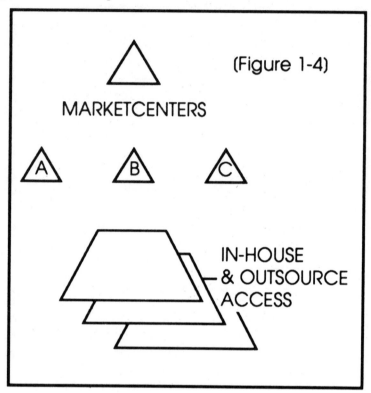

cess to products that are not self-manufactured? Figure 1-6
shows an enterprise model composed of three marketcenters
headed by Pyramidless Peaks. The consultancies at the peaks
can do business with their in-house manufacturers, or they
can go outside, mixing and matching their applications to get
the best deals—that is, to supply the most cost-effective
outcomes.

Visualizing Customer Asset Bases as Markets

Your customers are not companies. They are managers of
customer operating processes whose contributions to their
companies' profits can be improved by your applications.

Some of your customers may run cost-centered business functions. Others may run profit-centered lines of business.

In order to become a function manager's preferred provider—not as a supplier of products or services but as a provider of improved contributions to the manager's profit-making capabilities—you must be process-smart in the key work flows that you can affect. The added values of your applications-smarts depend on how well you can apply them to answer questions such as these:

- How much is a business function or line of business currently contributing to customer growth, either negatively by adding cost or positively by adding revenues and earnings?
- Where do the critical costs cluster in each process? What are the critical success factors in each process that contributed the most to revenues?
- How much improvement can you bring by applying the single best solution to a cost problem or a revenue opportunity and how long will it take for the customer to realize the improvement?
- How much net added value does your improvement allow the business-function manager or line-of-business manager to contribute to his or her company as the outcome of your application?

The answer to the last question has three important ramifications. One, its value represents your "product," which is what you are selling. Two, it forms the value-base for your price because it represents what your customers are "buying" from you. Three, it defines your business by specifying what you do best and what you do better than your competitors.

Which customer processes contain the assets you choose to enhance? Are you an improver of design and development processes—an accelerator of their innovation cycles and an enhancer of the commercial values of each new product or service?

Are you an improver of manufacturing processes—an accelerator of their production or testing cycles, an integrator of their systems, an improver of their time to market, a reducer of their costs, and an enhancer of their quality?

Are you an improver of sales and marketing processes—an accelerator of their selling cycles, an expander of their markets or their shares within markets, a booster of their volume or margins, or a reducer of their distribution costs?

The customer processes you choose to affect—whether you sell your applications into them or integrate their workflow systems or re-engineer their operations or become your customers' co-manager of them—determines what kind of business you own. If you make your primary impact on customer cost centers by helping their managers avoid, reduce, or eliminate cost outcomes, you are going to be perceived as a cost-reducer. If you make your primary impact on customer profit centers by helping their managers speed up or add to their revenue or margin outcomes, you are going to be perceived as a revenue-builder.

These outcome-driven perceptions of your impacts act as shorthand definitions of your business and what you are "good at." They complete your customers' vision of you as "the people who..."

Achieving Constructive Monopoly

Managing your business "like you own it" means more than owning stewardship of the business you manage. It means owning your business category to such an extent that you are a constructive monopoly—that is, you preempt the preference of your heaviest profit-contributing customers by becoming their most-preferred provider of optimal outcomes.

Preemptive control of your market's preference is the legal way to achieve monopoly pricing at high margins. High margins flow to you not because you control a means of production but because you dominate a means of customer satisfaction. This is the only enduring strategy for market control. It endows the value of your outcomes with brand status. By downgrading your competitors to number two or worse, you reduce them to commodities. They are forced to adopt a reactive position, enabling you to predict and counteract their strategies.

Once you become your market's standard-bearer of value, all of your competitors compare unfavorably against you. You do not have to make these comparisons. Your customers make them for you. This is why your monopoly is "constructive": It exists *de facto* in the minds of your customers rather than *de jure*.

Becoming dominant as a quasi-monopolist comes from using your capabilities to make your customers dominant in their own markets. Your business growth opportunity is directly proportional to the degree and continuity of dominance you confer on your core customers.

Customer enhancement, not enhanced product or service performance or quality, is the requisite for dominance. Even if you are "the best," saying so only makes you prominent, not dominant. You must be able to promise your customers that you can help *make them the best* as the result of doing business with you. The test of your dominance is the customers you make dominant. Their dependence on you to perpetuate their dominance is your only compelling grasp on them as their monopolist.

Turning your customers to dominance and returning them to doing business with you to maintain their dominance must be your prime business objectives. The faster you turn and return customers to dominant outcomes, the faster you can grow them. The faster you grow them, the faster they are able to grow you. In this way, your customers take you into ownership of your vision.

Part Two
Implementing Ownership

2
Own Applications

How Applications Interact With Margins and Productivity

For want of applications, improved customer outcomes are lost.

For want of improved customer outcomes, margins are lost.

For want of margins, the resources to continuously improve applications and increase their productivity are lost.

If you are going to manage your business "like you own it," you must be the applications king of your industry.

Nobody must be able to apply the products, services, or systems in your category to provide better outcomes for your customers by reducing critical costs or expanding profitable revenue streams.

High-quality products and services help to achieve quality outcomes. But if you have to make a choice, you are better off with a combination of parity products and superior applications skills. This combination makes sure that your customers can get all the value out of your products that you put into them. The other way around makes sure that they do not.

Applications seek functions. They are function-driven, function-specific, and function-improving. In a cost-centered business function, applications seek out costs they can reduce. In a customer's-profit-centered businesses, applications seek out new revenue potential they can wring out of sales, marketing, and distribution functions.

A customer function is an application's home. The matrix shown in Figure 2-1 is a way to make sure that your portfolio of applications knows where its homes are. When you fill it in, it gives you a bird's-eye view of your business.

If you think applications first and products and services second, you can screen new product investments and evaluate your current product and service lines through questions such as these:

- When this product or service is applied to a customer's business function, how much can it contribute in its planned or current format to making the customer a lower cost supplier? How significant will its contribution be? How reliable? How maintainable, repairable, or re-

Figure 2-1. Industry-specific applications/functions matrix.

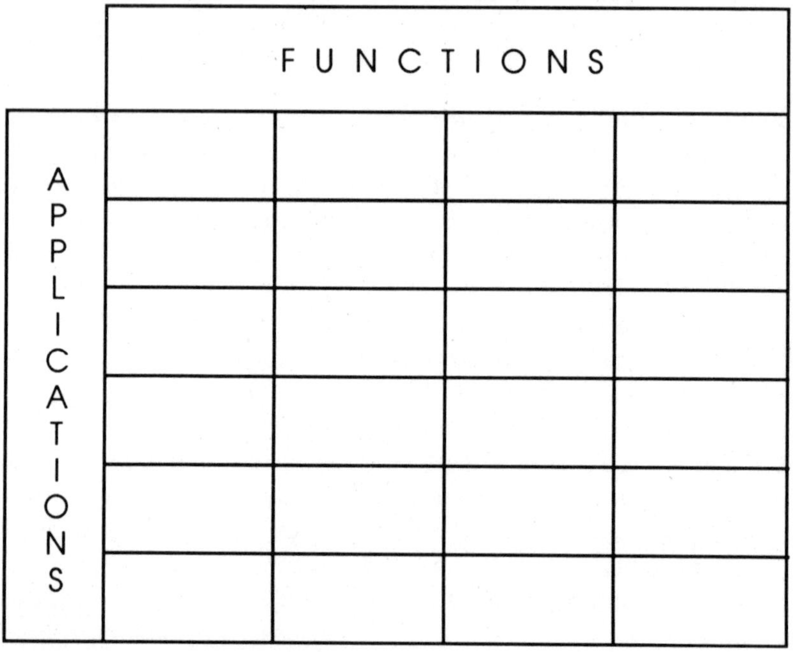

placeable? How integratable into current customer operations?

• When this product or service is applied to a customer's line of business, how much can it contribute in its planned or current format to making the customer a higher market-shareholder or higher-margin marketer? How significant will its contribution be? How reliable? How maintainable, repairable, or replaceable? How integratable into current customer operations?

Time and money are the two values from your applications that are marketable. Time and money saved, time and money gained. The time-and-money market is infinite; it knows no saturation point. Once a customer has acquired an asset base, he must commit to its continuous improvement. He may not be in the market for additional assets. But he or she must always be in the market for ways to manage current assets better, and for co-managers who can help.

When you try to "own applications" in your industry— that is, own the industry standard for the customers' outcomes you can affect—you cannot sell by asking customers if they need, want, or desire your products or services. In order to get at applications opportunities, you must learn where current outcomes fall short of conferring competitive advantage. "Falling short" means that current outcomes are unsatisfactorily costly, slow, undependable, or are leaving sales on the table because of a customer's failure to fully capitalize on market opportunity.

Getting at Applications Opportunities

If you get challenged on the way to penetrating a market with a "Halt! Who goes there?" from a prospective customer, your first few words are crucial. If you use them to position yourself as a bearer of assets in the form of your own products or services, you will be looked on as an added cost that will have to be added to even further by the customer's application skills in order to "get to outcome." But if you position yourself as an outcome-improver and feature the track record of your industry-standard applications skills, you can be looked on as a value bringer who can reduce—not add to—customer costs: a value bringer who can supplement, complement, and help implement the customer's applications skills. This requires you to translate the negative values of acquiring your assets into their applied benefit values.

The way to make this translation from cost-adder to value-adder is to target leads for applications opportunities by asking questions such as these:

- What is the current outcome of your forecasting process on inventory?
- What is the current outcome of your inventory process on same-day order fulfillment?
- What is the current outcome of your downtime cycle on shipments?
- What is the current outcome of your product development process on market share?
- What is the current outcome of your market databasing process on the allocation of advertising-and-promotion funds?
- What is the current outcome of your quality control process on repairs under warranty?
- What is the current outcome of your billing process on accounts-receivable collections?
- What is the current outcome of your manufacturing process on the cost-effectiveness of small production runs?
- What is the current outcome of your direct product-profitability analyzing process on the allocation of future funds?

By making each of your applications fit a targeted need for an improved outcome, you can be partner-specific for your customers. Is your customer base composed of brand managers of consumer packaged-goods companies? In order to be partner-specific for them, you must be able to improve their current outcomes from converting first-time tryers of their products into repeat purchasers. Is your customer base composed of manufacturing managers of high-technology companies? In order to be partner-specific for them, you must be able to improve their current outcomes from just-in-time inventory management or from flexible manufacturing systems or total quality programs.

How good do your applications skills have to be? The answer is a resolution of two factors that can make you "best of breed":

- Your outcomes must be better than a customer's current outcomes.
- Your outcomes must be better than your best competitor's outcomes.

The best outcome for an improved customer sales cycle or accounts-receivable collection cycle or new product development cycle may be only one month earlier than competition: If you own that one month, you own the application.

The best outcome for a customer's work shift productivity may be only one percent greater than competition. If you own that one percent, you own the application.

The best margin for a customer's "meal ticket" product may be only one dollar higher than competition. If you own that one dollar, you own the application.

What does it mean to "own" one month in receivables collection or one percent in productivity per work shift or one dollar in margin? It means that you have mastered the skill of making these outcomes happen, that you can be relied on to deliver them consistently, and that no one equals you or exceeds you or is more reliable than you. Owning the application means owning the franchise to install it. It means you have first refusal. It means that your name comes to mind immediately, as if it were hyphenated to the name of the application, and that nobody else's name comes close.

When you own the standards of outcome improvement for an application, you can challenge your customers to do better. "Your labor cost being contributed to this operation is $350,000," you can say; "What if we can help you get it down by 10 percent?" "Your materials cost contribution is $500,000 with 10 percent scrap; what if we can help you get it down to $450,000 with virtually zero scrap?" "Each new product is netting you an average of only $250,000 in its first commercial year; what if we can help you get it up to $300,000?"

Converting Technology Into Applications

Technology is to have and to hold, but not to sell. It is the source of your capabilities but not their outcome. Only outcomes from a technology, which means the results that take place in a customer's operations when you apply it, are marketable at high margins. If you manufacture technology, build your business around the outcomes from its applications and not around the technology itself. If you apply technology, do the same. Take pride in your technology, but keep both the pride and the technology to yourself.

When it comes to making margins, pride in a technology comes before the fall. As an asset, technology constitutes a cost to you. Your customers want to acquire its applied values, not your costs. Your technology may be a cause of your values. But your customers want the results from putting it to work for them.

You and your technical people will be in constant angst about which comes first: outcome pride or technology pride. Only if outcome pride wins will you be able to get your business synchronized with the businesses of your customers, who live and die based on their outcomes, not your technology. The protons, neutrons, or electrons that inhabit your technology are relevant only insofar as they contribute to reducing a customer cost or increasing revenues or earnings. Their relevance is determined by their contribution—and not their composition.

This lesson comes traditionally hard to technology suppliers. They learn it through their margins, an indisputable signal that science alone cannot elevate customer outcomes. Unfortunately, the signal comes only after the investment in science has already been sunk. Wall Street has made this discovery even while Silicon Valley has not. The stock market routinely discounts the value of technology the moment it is introduced, as it did when Hewlett-Packard announced a new computer chip technology. According to H-P, the technology would improve the performance of minicomputers and work stations by at least 70 percent. According to Wall Street: So what? The New York Stock Exchange dropped H-P's stock price $1.125 a share within twenty-four hours.

James Unruh, chairman of Unisys, has taken this fact of life to heart in restructuring his company around applications. "We were a business of selling technology," he says. "We've now evolved into a business of applying it." Figure 2-2 shows the stepladder of changes that Unisys has had to climb to "get to applications." Electronic Data Systems (EDS), on the other hand, began its business there. A Tier One business, it uses H-P and Unisys as a source of supply for its own applications.

Translating technology capabilities whose costs are negative values into the positive values of applied results that can be sold at high margins is a conversion process. If you skip it or do it poorly, you will never be able to translate your science into customer value; as a result, you will never be able to turn its technology into a business. Figure 2-3 shows three examples of how an asset base of flow technologies can be applied to make money. Figure 2-4 does the same for an asset base of propulsion technologies.

Read Figure 2-3 as if it spoke to you like this:

- Even if you have world-class carburetor technology, you are talking to yourself if you use up your sales cycle time by proclaiming your leadership in mastering the Venturi Effect. The only way to say something marketable about it is to translate your scientific capability into the customer outcomes it can improve when it is applied to measure and control the flow of gases in customer operations.
- Even if you have world-class microchip technology, the only way to say something marketable about it is to translate your scientific capability into the customer out-

Figure 2-2.   Unisys in transition.

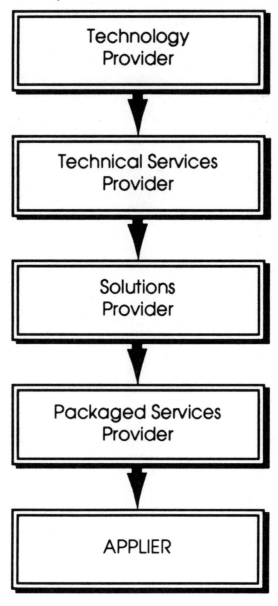

Figure 2-3. Applying flow technologies.

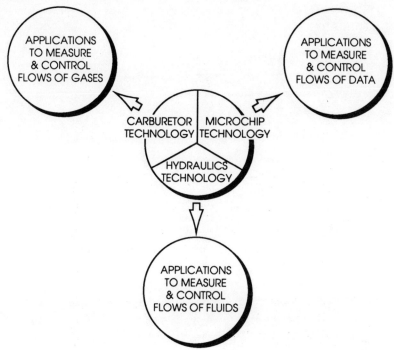

comes it can improve when it is applied to measure and control the flow of data in customer operations.
• Even if you have world-class hydraulics technology, the only way to say something marketable about it is to translate your scientific capability into the customer outcomes it can improve when it is applied to measure and control the flow of fluids in customer operations.

Read Figure 2-4 in a similar way for applying propulsion technologies.

It may take ceaseless repetition of this kind of marketese to make converts out of your technical people, or even yourself. But there is no choice. Your customers are not missionaries. They want you to come to them already converted. Your time-to-market cycle may depend on your technology. But

Figure 2-4. Applying propulsion technologies.

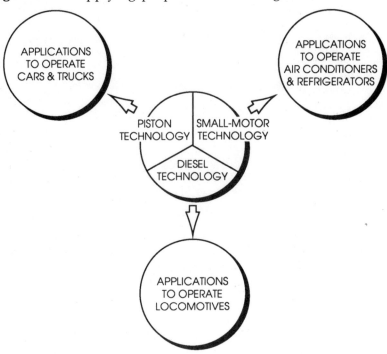

your time-to-close cycle when you sell depends on how quickly you can convert its capabilities into applied outcomes.

Going After the Innovator's Edge

"We've got a great idea," is not innovation.

Neither is "We've got an even better idea."

What is innovation? "We have a value that can be added to a customer operation in a cost-effective manner."

Applications are no different from products and services in their susceptibility to becoming commodities. Commodization happens as soon as their value can be replicated or exceeded. In one split second, they can lose their punch as prime outcome enhancers. When that takes place, your role as industry standard-bearer goes up for grabs.

In order to keep ahead of the wear-out curve, make innovation a three-pronged process:

1. You are always incrementally improving existing applications.
2. On a parallel track, you are always trying to obsolete each application with something better.
3. At the same time, you are carrying on true innovation that can rearrange the playing field rather than renovate what takes place on it.

Through this process, three new applications can come out of each existing one. The first two levels fund the third until it goes commercial. When it produces the innovator's profits, it pays back your investment in the entire process.

Before you make a run at innovator's profits, screen your thinking through a six-point Go/No-Go analysis to answer the key question: *Will it make a cost-effective improvement in customer outcomes?*

1. To which function will it make a contribution?
2. How much will it contribute?
3. How soon will the contribution be realized?
4. At what rate of return on investment?
5. How does the contribution compare with contributions from actual or predictable competitive innovations?

If you still feel good about it, ask the final question:

6. Is it cost-effective for *us*? Can we make high margins on it?

When you think about innovation, never ask: What can we do better or make in a different way? Ask instead: Which customer assets can we help manage better by *applying which capabilities to which functions* of customer businesses? Managing customers' assets innovatively, not selling them assets of your own such as products or services, is where the margins are. Whenever you can help a customer manage assets so that they make a lower contribution to costs or a higher contribution to revenues, you earn your margins as your share of the improvement in customer competitiveness. This is the only claim you can have on them.

If you want your profits from innovation to be continuous, you must be innovating all the time. Continuity is also necessary for another reason. Innovation is unpredictable. You cannot turn it on and off, hoping for a blockbuster to come out of the chute each time you open it. By making innovation continuous, you can take small incremental bites out of new application opportunities on a learn-as-you innovate/ innovate-as-you-learn basis.

A simple innovative strategy is more cost-effective than a strategy that periodically bets the business on a one-shot breakthrough. Breakthrough strategies try to produce elephants. But elephantine innovations defy implementation. They disrupt a customer's current operations. They require a customer's labor force to go back to school. They consume customer funds at the same time they interrupt cash flow. Innovation is much more manageable, as well as affordable, for both you and your customers when you think of its end product as an endless chain of linked elephant sausages rather than elephants.

Aiming at "Good Enoughness"

No customer wants his business continuity to be interrupted, let alone his critical processes to be made obsolete and his people's proficiencies nullified, by an innovation that cannot be incorporated into his ongoing operations. The ideal innovation fits easily into a customer's current work flows and can be integrated into them without a great deal of retraining, restructuring, or reengineering.

It is an unaffordable risk for you to disadvantage the continuity of customer operations no matter how much added future value you can claim for an innovation. The way to make innovation safe is to logically extend each incremental gain from what you already know is "your game." Figure 2-5 shows a model Game Grid, where "your game" is the most

Figure 2-5. Game Grid.

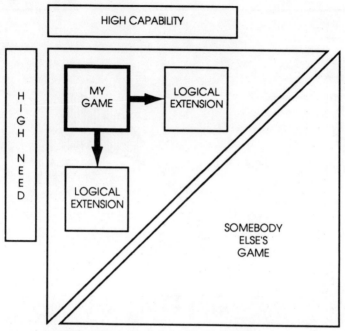

perfect fit between your customers' high-level needs and your own highest capabilities. "Your game" is Innovation Central for you, your home base.

One of the two best things you can do to make innovation safe is to take incremental short leads off your home base through innovations based on logical extensions of your capabilities. The second way to make innovation safe is to stop each improvement at the point where it is "good enough" to add the next most cost-effective increment to customer competitiveness. As Figure 2-6 shows, good enough is a customer's evaluation. It comes at the point where he judges himself to be satisfied with the new resolution you have given him between productivity and quality in return for his investment to achieve it.

Good enough means enough improvement to give a customer a more optimal outcome that is no less than what is

Figure 2-6.   Stopping at good enough.

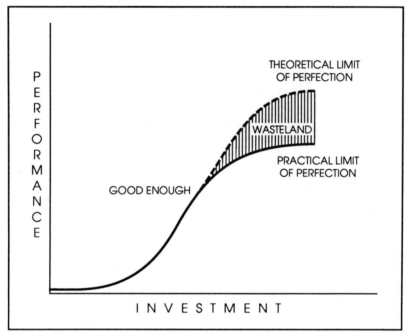

needed but no more than what can be used. In this sense, it provides all the competitive advantage necessary to maintain the best practices but only enough to do the job.

Value over and above good enough is overengineered, overcosted, and likely to be overpriced in relation to its contribution to outcome. That is why good enough is always an optimal improvement and never the maximum improvement.

In order to maximize customer improvement, you would have to invest time, talent, and money far beyond the good-enough point shown in Figure 2-6. This is a wasteland. Every man-day and every dollar of profits that you invest in this morass buys you proportionately less customer satisfaction and therefore less of a premium margin per unit of sale. If you were actually able to reach the theoretical limit of perfection, you would already have overshot the ability to reclaim your added costs. If you tried to incorporate them into your price, you would find that your investment in technological perfection deters sales, not attracts them.

If you press on to theoretical perfection at the six sigma level of 99.9997 out of 100, you tie up your best minds trying to eke out the final 20 percent of value that can cost you up to 80 percent of your total investment in an innovation. You also incur opportunity costs from your failure to make the next incremental innovation. Therefore, before you commit to total perfection, calculate the sales and profit differences between 99.9997 and 99.9996, and so on back down to good enough. The place to stop is the point at which further investment is no longer proportionately recoverable.

Continuously Improving Applications

A policy of continuous improvement helps you defend your business against missing a curve in applications development. A missing link in an evolutionary development schedule such as the one shown in Figure 2-7 may not put you out of business. But it will put you out of the premium-margin business and into the catch-up innovation business. Not only do you have to catch the curve you have missed; you have to run to catch the next curve so that you do not miss out on it as well. This puts excruciating pressure on your R&D. At the same time that you are furiously funding your developers, you have fewer premium-margin dollars to fund them with.

A good way to avoid missing curves is to manage improvement as a dual loop process, as Figure 2-8 shows. Your normal "extendo" loop helps you extend your current applications by progressively upgrading them. Concurrently, you initiate "innovo" loops: endless interruptions and alterations in your current asset base that continually invigorate it with new inspirations.

Innovo loops announce that it is politically correct to have a change-driven mindset that seeks to overthrow the existing order of "the way things are done" in your business, no matter how successful things are. Using the *kaizen* principle of

(text continues on page 54)

Figure 2-7. Missing a curve.

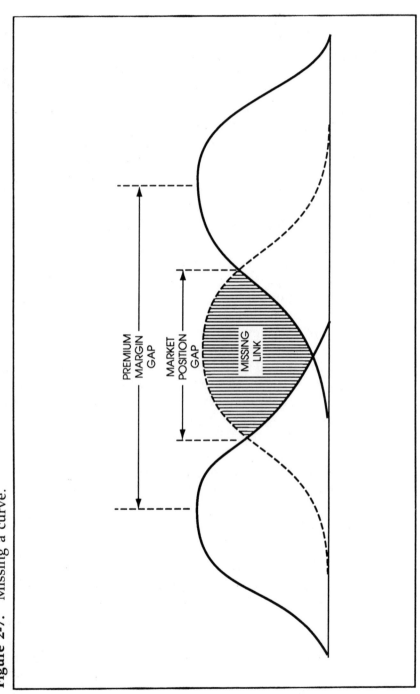

PREMIUM MARGIN GAP

MARKET POSITION GAP

MISSING LINK

Figure 2-8. Dual-loop innovation process.

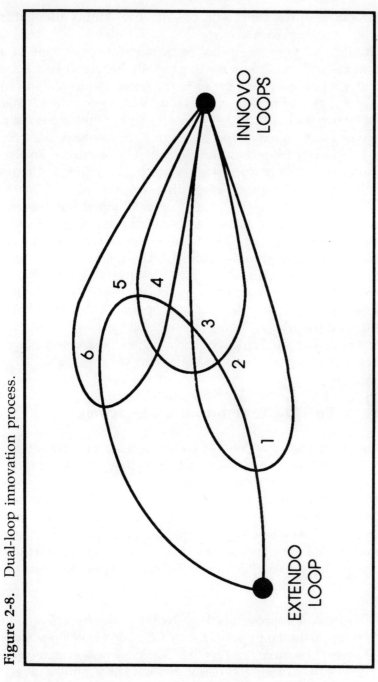

continuous improvement, you can make prodding the status quo into a mainstream activity.

It takes all your ingenuity to manage improvement as a continuous process. You have to get your people lined up for it—whipped up may be a better term. Texas Instruments used to have a group of in-house anarchists who were called "wild hares." Their job was to keep interrogating the status quo. They were wave-makers and pot-stirrers by executive decree. As a subsidized underground movement, they were able to get under-the-table financing in the form of Wild-Hare Grants for innovo-type business cases that confronted the mainstream way of doing business—or challenged established businesses themselves. Grants encouraged hot pursuit of strategy options that were unlikely to come out of perpetuating an extendo loop. The grants would see TI's wild hares through prototype development. After that, they faced Judgment Day.

Some companies call their anarchists "speculators." Others think of them as bootleggers who operate in a skunkworks-type of underworld. At IBM they are "Wild Ducks," who defy flying in formation. Whatever their names, anarchists play a necessary role as professional limit-testers.

Putting Your Brand on Outcomes

Continuous innovation keeps you "branded," preventing you from falling into commodity status as just another vendor whose sole differentiation is your price.

A brand is an application that produces a premium outcome. Based on its premium value, it can command a premium margin. As a result of an improved outcome, a customer's operation also becomes branded with its own competitive advantage. In the customer's industry, his operation can become "best of breed."

- If you can improve Black & Decker's sales by $15 million by applying an improved forecasting and inventory management system, and neither Black & Decker nor anyone else can achieve a superior outcome at a similar investment, you have branded your application. Black & Decker has also branded its forecasting and inventory operations as best practices in its industry.

- If you can save Heinz U.S.A. $200,000 by increasing order entry operations 75 percent, and neither Heinz nor anyone else can achieve a superior outcome at a similar investment, you have branded your application. Heinz has also branded its order entry operation as best practice in its industry.

Your brands are your margin-makers. Figure 2-9 shows how brands make money for you on their way up the life-cycle curve.

In a branded business, profits get out in front of sales. This is the result of high unit margins. Figure 2-10 shows the reverse effect. Once premium margins are lost to discounting,

Figure 2-9. Profit/sales relationship on the way up.

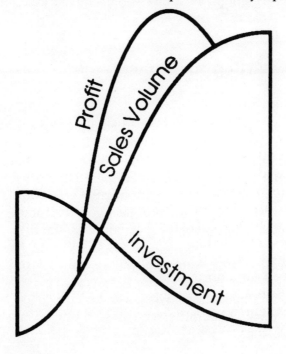

Figure 2-10.   Profit/sales relationship on the way down.

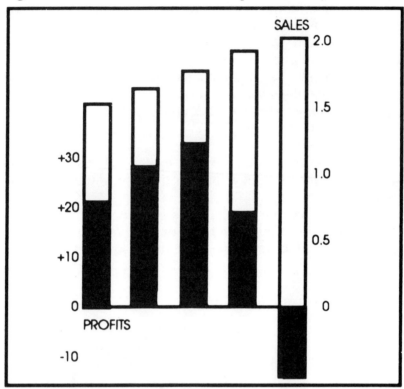

sales get out in front of profits. In a branded business, growth profits can quickly pay back your start-up investment and allow you to become self-capitalizing. After that, recurring investments can be funded from operating cash flows.

Along with being your moneymakers, brands are your business positioners. They preselect your customers according to who owns the outcomes that you can brand:

- If you brand your applications as cost reducers, you make your primary appeal to cost-center managers in mature businesses who will be compelled to partner with you to reduce the costs of one or more of their outcomes.

- If you brand your applications as revenue expanders, you make your primary appeal to profit-center managers of three types of businesses who will be compelled to partner with you to stimulate their sales outcomes in one or more of their lines of business:
  —Growth businesses that they want to keep growing at an accelerated rate
  —Start-up businesses that they want to get into a growth mode by penetrating their markets quickly
  —Mature businesses that they want to regrow

The natural law of business ensures that brands are a roll of the dice. Out of every eight attempts at innovation, you are likely to end up with the mixed bag of results shown in Figure 2-11:

- One branded Big Winner, shown as number 4
- Two branded Profit Makers, shown as 5 and 6

Figure 2-11. Brand distribution.

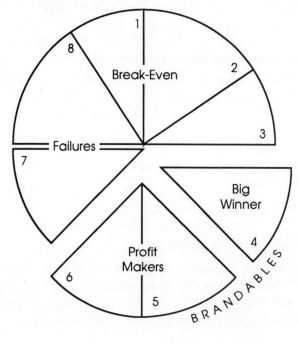

- Three Breakevens, shown as 1, 2, and 3
- Two Failures, shown as 7 and 8

The proportion of break-evens and failures may switch back and forth because a failure can net out at only one dollar below the earnings required for it to break even. But the single big winner out of eight is hardly ever exceeded.

The best advice for managing continuous innovation is to adopt a policy of *triage*: Accentuate the positive, eliminate the negative, and don't mess with Mr. In-Between.

1. *Accentuate the positive.* Allocate a disproportionately large amount of assets to your brandable Big Winner and Profit Makers. Assign your best managers to them. Support them with your best teams. Incent them with the highest rewards. Go for broke.

2. *Eliminate the negative.* Cut your losses. Get out of your failures as quickly as you identify them, and reallocate their assets to your brandable Big Winner and Profit Makers. Make the mistake of getting out too soon rather than too late. Like successes, most failures announce themselves early. Avoid the tendency to rationalize an "eight barrel pumper"—as a submarginal well is called in the oil patch—into a nine with the hope that it can become a ten some day.

3. *Don't mess with Mr. In-Between.* It is easier to get out of losers and let your winners run than it is to know how to deal with break-even businesses that are borderline Profit Makers or Failures. The longer you deficit-finance them, the less likely it is that they will ever pay you back. Make them declare themselves one way or the other by provoking them with three strategies:

a. Retarget their market.
b. Rebalance their value-to-price relationship.
c. Refocus their promotion.

In-between products and services are in between for a reason. They are usually positioned in between markets in "No Man's Land," where there is no market. By rebalancing their value-price relationship and refocusing their promotion, you can feel around quickly to see if something is really there or if you need to get out. Make the same mistake you make with your Failures: Get out one quarter too soon rather than one quarter too late. Even when you are wrong, you will be wrong for the right reason.

Optimizing Customer Asset Management

The marketing benefit of owning applications is that you can focus your customers' attention on their own operations, not on yours. Instead of being an alternate product or service vendor to your customers, you can take on the role of their investment advisor who can improve the competitiveness of customer assets under your co-management. If you make products, you are relieved of the need to sell them the traditional way, feature by feature, benefit by benefit, and discount by discount. Instead, you can sell the outcomes of applying products and their support services to speed up a customer's production or reduce time and money currently going to waste by manufacturing a high percentage of scrap.

If you can increase a customer's productivity by 30 to 40 percent by reducing downtime, you can make more money by basing your price on the value of the improved productivity than by pricing the products or services that contribute to the improved outcome. If you can reduce a customer's change-over time on a product redesign from nine hours down to seven, you can make more money by basing your price on the value of the improved time-to-market than by pricing the products or services that contribute to the improved outcome. If you can increase a customer's trial-to-repurchase ratio by 20 percent, or the percentage of orders filled the same day they are received by 35 percent, or the number of inventory turns by 10 percent, you can make more money by gainsharing the improved values than by pricing the contributing products or services.

When you go to market, you have to know what to say about yourself. If you are a supplier of health care systems, you must bite your tongue to make sure that you say nothing

about the systems themselves until you have said what the
outcome will be from applying them to reduce your hospital
customers' costs or increase your home care customers' revenues. If you are a supplier of computer systems, you must
say nothing about the systems themselves until you have said
what the outcome will be from applying them to reduce your
customer's downtime costs.

In some cases, the assets you will be dealing with are
undermanaged by your customers. In other cases, they are
overmanaged or mismanaged. Your way of doing business is
to manage outcome-improvement projects that improve a
customer's contribution from his assets. In this way, your
customers' improved standards of performance will make you
the owner of applications.

3
Own Margins

**How Margins Interact
With Applications and Productivity**

For want of margins, profits are lost.

For want of profits, the resources to continuously improve internal productivity are lost.

For want of improved internal productivity, the ability to generate a steady state of improved applications is lost.

If you are going to manage your business "like you own it," you must be the Margin King of your industry.

Nobody must merit higher margins for applying your category of products, services, and systems to the customer functions or lines of business that you affect because nobody must be able to provide better outcomes. Your margins are your share of the gain your customers realize from having some of their critical costs reduced or some of their profitable revenue streams expanded.

Margin management is the only definition of management. What else is there to manage for? Why else are you a manager? Anyone can give margins away.

Your margins prove three things about you as a manager:

1. Margins prove your brands. Low margins or no margins prove commodities.
2. Margins prove your value. Low margins or no margins prove that you provide low value, no value, or unknown value.

3. Margins prove who owns your business. Low margins
    or no margins prove that your competitors and cus-
    tomers are your absentee owners.

Figure 3-1 shows how to make margins. If you run your
business on curve 1 of the figure, where you sell products or
services on their price and performance, you earn low or no
margins. This is your customers' way of compensating themselves for the added costs you represent. On curve 2, you
represent an additional cost for advice, unless you can prove
that it delivers a value greater than the price you charge for it.

Curve 3 is where margins are made at their highest levels.
When you run your business on curve 3, you position yourself
as a co-manager of customer assets. Your co-management
skills improve the contributions that customer assets can make
to customer profits. Your margins are your gainshare. They

Figure 3-1. Maximizing margin potential.

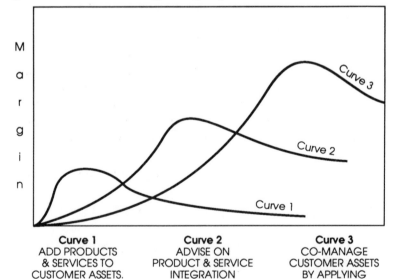

reward you in proportion to the amount of improvement you contribute.

On curve 3, you may be a supplier of products or services. Or you may be an integrator of other suppliers' products or services, acting as their general contractor to bring the optimal mix together for each project in just the right way at just the right time. In either case, your true product consists of the value from applying your intellectual capital—your applications-smarts—to the products and services that you install in a customer's asset base. The value shows up in the improved performance of the customer outcomes you contribute to.

Discounting your margins proves that you are on curve 1. Either you are contributing no added value over and above your cost, or you do not know your value. If your customers have calculated your value and you are still required to discount your margins, they are using knowledge that you should have in order to double-dip into your profits. Think of this as a tax on your ignorance: taxation without representation of value.

Doing "Good Deals"

As an owner-manager, your day-to-day agenda is to do good deals. You deal to make more money for your business by enabling it to make more money or save more money for your customers. Every time you deal a dollar, you should question letting it leave your hand by challenging yourself in this way:

- Can these dollars yield the added revenues or reduced costs that I need?
- Can I get the same amount of added revenues or reduced costs cheaper?
- Can I get them faster?
- Can I get them at a lower risk?

Because money makes money, owner-managers run their businesses by running a continuous investment-return-reinvestment cycle. Money must keep turning over all the time. Money at rest certifies a dead business. The higher your margins, the more you have to invest. The faster each investment is returned, the faster you can reinvest it. The greater the return, the more you can reinvest.

The art of managing money—which is another way of saying moving it—is to keep your capital funds continuously employed in investments that generate operating income. Some investments generate more, others less. But all investments are good deals as long as their discounted cash flows add up to more than the cost of the capital you put in. The greater the gap between the capital you put in and the cash flows you get out, the better the deal. The gap is your margin.

If there are any tricks of the trade in maximizing your cash flows, you will find them in the following checklist of incremental investment criteria:

- The primary objective is long-term capital appreciation.
- The focus is on total return—the aggregate return from capital appreciation.
- The emphasis is on consistency of growth by avoiding volatility in annual values.
- Total return must meet or exceed a minimum IRR (incremental rate of return) of 100 percent.
- Minimize the capital invested in each project.
- Keep capital continuously employed.

Good deal making requires that each deal must maximize its return. Four criteria are worth pasting to your bathroom mirror to help you remember what a good deal looks like when one comes along:

1. It improves contribution margin.
2. It improves inventory or receivables turnover.
3. It improves circulation of capital.
4. It reduces, eliminates, or displaces costs.

Improving Contribution Margin

Contribution margin is what remains of sales revenues after your variable costs to produce them have been subtracted. Whatever is left over contributes to paying off fixed overhead costs and accounting for your operating profits.

There are three ways to improve the contribution margin of your business. One is to increase sales volume at the current margin. Another is to increase the margin contributed by each dollar of sales at the current volume. The third is to reduce your variable costs so there is less to subtract from sales revenues.

Improving Turnover

Turnover measures the rate of flow of your capital funds as they circulate in a complete cycle from cash through inventory to receivables, and then back again to cash to start the next cycle.

Inventory turnover is calculated by the number of months' supply on hand. A six-months' supply of a product that turns two times a year equals a 200 percent annual turnover. Receivables turnover is calculated by the number of days' worth of receivables outstanding. If 90 days are outstanding and receivables turn four times a year, your receivables turn is 400 percent.

By reducing either inventory or receivables, you reduce the amount of your funds invested in working assets. This reduces your total asset base, which reduces the amount of fixed costs that must be absorbed by your margins.

Improving Circulating Capital

Capital increases with each turn it circulates, driven by your sales. Operating profits can be improved by increasing sales, increasing margins on sales, reducing your cost of sales, or reducing general and administrative expenses.

Your capital is composed of accounts receivable, inventory, and net investment. You can calculate your return on capital with the ROCE (return on capital employed) formula:

$$\frac{\text{Profit before taxes}}{\text{Capital employed}}$$

Reducing Costs

The three major contributors to costs in product-based businesses are labor, materials, and inventory. Service businesses are cost-intensive in their inventory of labor. There are three strategies to reduce costs: avoid or postpone them; eliminate some portion of them; or displace them by leasing instead of buying, buying instead of making, or taking on partnered cosponsors as joint funders.

Good deals can become bad deals overnight unless you are constantly on guard against insufficient revenues or earnings and unnecessary or unaffordable costs.

Revenue problems typically come from unexpected deficiencies or interruptions in your cash flow. These can come from sales falloffs or delinquencies in billings and collections. In turn, these problems come from discounting your margins too heavily, being late to market, shipping and billing or collecting late, being out of stock and running behind in same-day order fulfillment, or misdirecting your promotions to nonmarkets.

Cost problems typically come from failing to maximize the capabilities in your asset base yet paying for them anyway, or failing to get rid of avoidable costs or reduce unnecessary ones. In turn, these problems come from low productivity, carrying excess inventory, too much downtime or overtime, too much scrap, and excessively high rates of returned goods or repairs under warranty.

Managing Contribution Margin

Of all the rules for making money, no rule is more important than "Watch your contribution margins." Are they growing?

Are they growing fast enough to stay ahead of your costs? Are they growing steadily? Are their sources changing?

Figures 3-2 through 3-4 show three ways to look at your contribution margins. Figure 3-2 shows contribution margin in operating-statement terms. Figure 3-3 shows contribution margin in relation to the lines of business that generate it. Figure 3-4 shows contribution margin in relation to sales.

Keep in mind that volume is not growth. Revenues can increase (and often do) while profits decline. You can show a loss at the same time you report an increase in revenues. Only profits pay off. Everything you do must contribute to profits. Sales force incentives should be profit-based instead of based on volume. Products should be niched, even microniched, to their market segments, so that they can earn higher margins from specialization. The greatest amount of your time should be spent managing the interrelationships between your volume, its costs, and the resulting contribution margin.

The life-cycle stage of your business will make a significant difference in your margin contribution:

• *At Your Start-up Stage.* In a new business with zero sales and $30 million in fixed costs as your start-up asset base, your contribution margin is zero. Your business reports a loss of $30 million.

• *Throughout Your Incremental-Growth Stage.* The loss declines as your business approaches break-even, which occurs at about 35 million units in sales. Beyond break-even, your contribution margin begins to flow into the business. At 5 million units, contribution margin is $50 million. After your $30 million fixed-cost burden is absorbed, profits of $20 million can accrue. The incremental sale of an additional 2 million units at the same variable cost increases your contribution margin to $70 million and doubles your profits to $40 million.

Just by knowing your margin, you can predict where you are in your business life cycle. Margin-watchers know the signs to look for. Synoptics Communications, a computer component supplier, once reported a 248 percent increase in

(text continues on page 71)

Figure 3-2. Contribution margin in operating-statement terms.

Sales (50,000 units @ $80)	$4,000,000	100.0 %
Cost of Goods Manufactured and Sold:		
Variable Manufacturing Costs		
(50,000 units @ $10)	500,000	12.5
Manufacturing Contribution Margin	3,500,000	87.5 %
Selling and Administrative Expense:		
Variable Selling and Administrative		
Expenses (50,000 units @ $5)	250,000	6.25
Contribution Margin	$3,250,000	81.25%

Figure 3-3. Contribution margin by line of business.

	Total	A	B	C	D
Number of Units Sold	396,000	32,000	100,000	84,000	180,000
Selling Price per Unit	$14.80AV	$15.00	$8.00	$16.00	$18.00
Variable Manufacturing Cost*	6.06AV	9.80	4.90	9.60	4.49
Variable Selling and Administrative Expense	.57AV	1.00	.18	1.00	.50
Contribution Margin	$ 8.17AV	$ 4.20	$2.92	$ 5.40	$13.10

Total Fixed Costs	$1,726,000

Note: AV = average of product lines
*Materials, factory supplies, labor, other variable costs

Figure 3-4. Contribution margin in relation to sales.

Product Line	% Total Sales	% Product Line Contribution Margin on Sales	% Product Line Contribution Margin to Total
A	8.2	27.9	4.1
B	13.6	36.5	9.0
C	22.9	33.8	14.0
D	55.3	72.8	72.9
Total	100.0	52.2*	100.0

*Average contribution margin on total sales

quarterly profits on sales that were up 120 percent. But the margin-watchers saw a "slight erosion" in gross margins. The stock lost 16 percent of its value the same day.

Monitoring Your Margin Management

Your business has two sets of vital signs that you must monitor continuously in order to diagnose how well you are managing your margins:

- Your profitability, which reflects your margin muscle
- Your business activity, which acts as the multiplier of your margins

Each set of the vital signs consists of several ratios:

Profitability Ratios

Gross profit ratio	= Gross profit/sales
Net income to sales	= Net income/sales
Percent profit on sales	= Net profit/sales
Return on investment (ROI)	= Net income/total assets

Activity Ratios

Inventory turnover	= Sales/inventory
Day's sales in inventory	= 365 days/inventory turnover
Accounts-receivable turnover	= Credit sales/accounts receivable
Collection period (days)	= 365 days/accounts-receivable turnover
Investment turnover	= Net sales/total investment

If you have trouble keeping an eye on so many indicators, concentrate on just two: percent profit on sales and investment turnover.

Percent Profit on Sales

Profit as a percentage of sales is an index of how well you are adjusting the critical mix between your sales volume and the costs of producing it. You can calculate percent profit on sales by dividing net profit by sales:

$$\frac{Net\,profit}{Sales} = Percent\ profit\ on\ sales$$

The answer to the question, "Are you growing the business?" is not "Yes, I am growing sales." The only viable answer is, "Yes, I am growing profit as a percentage of sales—I am growing my margins."

Investment Turnover

Since your business is based on invested assets, your profits must exceed them or their costs will take you down. Growth depends on getting your capital investment to circulate fast. You can calculate investment turnover by dividing net sales by total investment, which is the same as dividing them by total assets:

$$\frac{Net\ sales}{Total\ investment} = Percent\ investment\ turnover$$

Increasing sales is paramount in maximizing the turnover of your invested capital. Margin management is primarily sales-growth management. Yet sales growth must always be balanced by reducing or at least limiting the total operating investment in the business at the same time that sales are being increased. Growth is not more sales. Growth is more profitable sales.

Profitable sales have two natural enemies. One is your cost of sales. The other is discounting.

Cost of sales comes right out of your revenues. Your gross sales margins are calculated by subtracting cost of sales from sales. Manufacturing, marketing, unsold inventory, and selling expenses compose your cost of sales. Their control is essential to margin management. Suppose you have a 20 percent net margin, which represents the profits that are left after all your costs are paid up. Every $1,000 in sales yields $200. A 10 percent increase in sales will add $20 to your profits. You can add another $80 if you can reduce your cost of sales by 10 percent. Every reduction in costs of 2.5 percent adds the same profits as each 10 percent increase in sales.

Discounting is a margin killer. Look what happens if you discount your margins by only 10 percent:

- If you have a 50 percent margin—the kind of margin that your customers say you'll never miss a piece of—you must increase sales by 25 percent to realize your original contribution. To do this, you have to raise your cost of sales.
- If you have a 35 percent margin, you must sell 40 percent more.
- If you have a 20 percent margin, you must sell 100 percent more.

Under duress, Compaq Computer put these ratios to the test. In order to gain market share in the commodity PC business, Compaq cut prices of its personal computers by an average of 32 percent across the board. Its gross margins fell by the same amount. Net operating margins went down to 5 percent from their former high of 18 percent. As a result, Compaq had to squeeze $225 million out of its costs. The easiest place to do it was the work force, which was reduced by a quarter.

Basing Price on Outcome

When you own an application, it can be more profitable than owning a patent on a product or a process. Owning the application area of inventory management gives you a blank check to go anywhere in your customer markets and save unnecessary costs they are incurring for insurance, security, and warehousing facilities. At the same time you are saving them money, you can also help your customers make money by optimizing their inventory mix so that they can move more of their best-selling products through distribution on the same day they are ordered.

If you own the application area of product development, you can go anywhere in your customer markets and save unnecessary design and development costs while also helping your customers make money by getting new products to market faster.

Owning an application rewards you with enhanced profit-making power in return for helping to enhance a customer's own power to make more profits. Whenever an application's outcome reduces a customer operation's contribution to cost, the savings can generally drop dollar for dollar to the customer's bottom line. Whenever an application's outcome increases sales turnover or profit margin on sales, the incremental revenues show up first on the customer's top line and then work their way down to the bottom line as residual earnings. The more costs you help a customer reduce, the more bottom-line earnings can be extracted from top-line revenues.

The customer costs you help reduce and the revenues and earnings that your applications help increase can become the basing points for your prices. Value-based pricing positions your customer outcomes as a "return on your price." Price becomes an investment that yields the return. Whatever the nature of your business, pricing based on the value of your customers' improved outcomes gives you the attribute of an asset co-manager. Your price is pay for performance. Your performance is improving the value of customer assets. If you guarantee the value of the asset improvements you contribute, your customers will underwrite your price. Your ability to guarantee your outcomes makes customer decision making automatic. One way or another—you make it happen or you make up the difference—the customer realizes his outcome.

As a co-manager of customer assets, your pricing formula is based on the net value of the improvement in the asset base you help manage. You can calculate your optimal price points with three guidelines:

1. Price should be within the customer's comfort zone for the cost of buying capital, as specified by the customer's hurdle rate.
2. Price should be within the customer's comfort zone for the expected payout, in comparison to competitive investment opportunities that bear similar levels of risk.
3. Price should be within the customer's comfort zone for payback of an investment within the customer's patience period.

The price you put on the value you contribute to customer outcomes is the single most important decision you can make in managing a business. It determines your profits. It also quantifies the worth of the assets that compose your core capabilities.

If you do not know the value you contribute, or if you underestimate it, you will underprice your applications. You will end up selling their applied value beneath its true worth. As a result, you will bring down on your business an unaffordable—and wholly unnecessary—opportunity cost.

You have a choice: Either contribute more value by applications than by discounting or say good-bye to your margins. Applied value is your ticket to earning a share of the outcomes you contribute to. But a customer will punch your ticket only if you can stand up to the kind of close-order drill that goes like this:

1. A customer demands a 10 percent discount.
2. You calculate that the money he will save is the equivalent of a 2 percent reduction in customer manufacturing costs. You can do better for him and do better for yourself by preserving your margins.
3. By reducing his labor content 10 percent, you can give the customer an 8 percent reduction in manufacturing costs. The equivalent discount to achieve the same cost reduction would have to be in the 40 percent range.
4. If you base your price on the value of reducing the customer's manufacturing costs—not on reducing his

purchase cost—you are able to enhance your margins as your share in the gain.

In this scenario, margin preservation is your reward for growing customer outcomes. It acts like a service fee in return for your management of customer assets in an improved manner—your fee for creating capital in the form of new funds. Unlike a discounted price, which is a *cause* of customer value, outcome-based prices are the *result* of value. The more value you add and the more quickly and consistently you add it, the higher your margins can be.

When you base price on value, price becomes a floating point. Price books become artifacts. List prices disappear. Without a price list, there is nothing to discount from. As you make each incremental contribution to customer outcomes, you can negotiate your price around the value it pays for. This is the strategy for maximizing your absolute profitability.

Absolute profitability tells you how much of a money-maker you are. Comparative profitability tells you how you measure up to your competitors. Four quick-and-dirty comparisons let you test your competitiveness:

1. Unit margin
2. Unit price
3. Unit volume
4. Unit cost

You want to be among the highest scorers in each of the first two measurements, no higher than you have to be in the third, and among the lowest in the fourth. How do you get there? You monitor the key price and cost elements that contribute to your comparative profitability.

In terms of how my pricing contributes to profitability compared to my competitors:

☐ Am I setting higher objectives than my competitors for the continuous improvement of customer outcomes? Am I measuring their achievement?

☐ Am I customizing function-specific solutions for each market segment to maximize customer outcomes over my competitors?

☐ Am I achieving my proposed outcomes within time frames that are faster than my competitors?

☐ Am I maintaining margin leadership by introducing more-frequent incremental innovations that add more measurable value to customer outcomes than my competitors?

In terms of how my costs contribute to profitability compared to my competitors:

☐ Am I focusing on a small number of core competencies so that I can minimize my asset base while maximizing my resource utilization for greater productivity than my competitors?

☐ Am I concentrating on narrow lines of business that are supplemented by more and better buy-vs-make decisions, joint ventures, and strategic alliances than my competitors?

☐ Am I decentralizing my organization so that I empower more decisions at lower operating levels than my competitors?

☐ Am I integrating more of my work flows and minimizing their cycle times more than my competitors?

☐ Am I maintaining better cost control by introducing incremental innovations that are small enough to be affordable at a frequency that is planned to avoid hurry-up or last-minute cost overruns?

Planning a High-Margin Business

If you plan a high-margin business from the outset, you can have the "Tom Kelley advantage." As manager of the Minnesota Twins baseball team, Kelley noticed that "You have to make four or five major decisions a game and a bunch of little decisions." If you make the major decisions right, the little decisions do not matter. If you make the major decisions wrong, the little decisions do not matter either.

The four major decisions you must make are all designed to help you perform your main job of margin management:

1. *Which customers should I plan to grow?* This tells you your market, the owners of your outcomes.
2. *What added value must I deliver to them?* This tells you your objectives, the source of your margins.
3. *What profit-improvement projects are the most cost-effective appliers of my added values?* This tells you your strategies, your application projects.
4. *What measurement system must I install to monitor each project's values?* This tells you your controls, your assessment process.

In your role as an asset co-manager for your customers, you must first grow the assets of each customer before growth can be returned to you. From the customer's perspective, win-win is always I-win-first.

This is also why you must plan first for the *outcome* of each customer's return and then, by derivation, for the *income* you can share as the result of your customer's outcome. Outcome and income objectives are always specified in dollar amounts because words are meaningless: Being the Low-Cost Producer or Market-Share Leader or Total-Quality Recordholder is not an objective. At worst, they are self-serving fluff. Only when you put numbers on them can they become objectives.

You want to be prepared for your four or five major decisions a game. You have a choice: deal with them ad hoc as they come up or plan for them in advance by What If-ing 20 percent of your total management time into playing futures:

- What unplannable events am I most likely to run into?
- What options am I most likely to have?
- What if I choose this one or that—which is more likely to give me the better outcome?

Playing futures is the ultimate management game. Never leave home without a supply of blank cost-benefit analysis forms on which to doodle What-Ifs, in the manner of Figure

Figure 3-5. Doodled cost-benefit analysis.

		Year 0 (Now)	Year 1	Year 2	Year 3
1	New Equipment Investment $	[17,750]			
2	Revenue		—	—	—
3	System Cash Saving		19,988	19,988	19,988
4	Non cash expense				
5	Depreciation ACRS		(2,525)	(3,710)	(3,541)
6	Material Trade In		10,000		
7	Profit Improvement BIT [3-5+6]		27,459	16,278	16,447
8	Less Income Tax 46%		(12,131)	(7,488)	(7,526)
9	Investment Tax Credit 10%		1,775		
10	Net Profit Improvement [7-8+9]		16,603	8,790	8881
11	CASH FLOW [1+5+10]	[17,500]	19,132	12,500	12,422
12	PAY BACK (cum. cash flow)	[17,500]	1,382	13,882	26,304
13					
14	Present Value - 10% factor	1.0000	.9516	.8611	.7791
15	Discounted Cash Flow [11×14]	(17,500)	18,206	10,764	9,678
16	Net Present Value Cash Flow [15]	37,828			
17					
18	Return On Investment [11÷1]		94%	50%	50%

3-5. You will throw most of them away. Try to throw them where your competitors can find them. When one looks good, add it to your plan.

When you play What-If, base your doodles on safe assumptions like these:

- Objectives always take longer to achieve than plan.
- When achieved, growth objectives always fall short of plan.
- Growth objectives always cost more than plan.
- Margins always erode faster than plan.
- Replicative competition always occurs earlier than plan.
- Market share always falls short of plan.
- Product and service line extensions always yield less than the original products and services.
- Resources always continue to be allocated beyond their point of maximum return.

- Changes in customer partners always occur at the worst times.
- Conservative judgment is always threatened by success.

Planning Inward and Backward

The growth of your business has two drivers:

1. *Your markets,* which is why you must grow them first so that they can grow you. Growth should therefore be planned from the market *inward* to your own business rather than outward to your markets.
2. *The future,* since all growth takes place after investment. Growth should therefore be planned from the future *backward* to the present rather than forward to the future.

Inward-and-backward planning begins with answering four questions:

1. What is the minimum requisite profit position for each of our major customers three years, two years, and one year from now?
2. What is the most likely contribution we can make to each position?
3. What is the minimal strategy mix we must invest to achieve each contribution?
4. What is the maximum share of the gain we can claim in return for contributing our value?

These questions constitute the essence of "backcasting," the inward-and-backward growth-planning process. The process originates with the market's future. Either your plan helps each of your customers realize the future that they are planning for and thereby becomes the Siamese twin of their own plan or it—and your business—risks being irrelevant to your sole sources of growth. Being relevant, on the other hand, means that you can get your prices up based on the value of your contribution and you can get your costs down by minimizing the investment in assets that you must manage in order to make your planned contribution.

Traditional forward planning as shown in Figure 3-6 gives you an entirely different set of plans. You tend to answer the question "How much must we grow?" by saying, "As much as possible," and "More." Instead of planning continuous incremental gain, you are tempted to go all out to achieve best-case objectives. But best case is pure chance, so much so that it actually works out to be the least likely case.

In planning forward, starting with your own capabilities first, you tend to answer the question "What strategies must we fund?" by saying, "All of them." You are tempted to overengineer and overcost them. You are tempted to give the same answer to the question "How much quality must we put into them?" You can never know the right answers. You never know what works or why. If you are successful, you are unlikely to cut back in order to find the minimal mix. If it is not working, you want to throw everything up for grabs for the same reason.

Forward plans are never any better than your skill in forecasting, a notoriously self-deceptive pseudoscience. It is entirely based on probabilities that can be negated in one stroke by a single major improbability or by a few minor ones that coincide. Fortunately, forward planning is only the first of three points of departure you can take to the planning process:

1. *Prospective,* which is the basis of forward planning when you start the process by asking, *"What is most likely to happen?"*
2. *Predictive,* when you start out by asking, *"What has already happened that will forecast the future?"*
3. *Retrospective,* where you start out by asking, *"What must have had to have happened in order to realize this future outcome?"*

Retrospective planning is the basis for inward-and-backward planning. As shown in Figure 3-7, retrospection begins at the end of year three of a three-year plan. It starts with the sum

(text continues on page 84)

Figure 3-6. Forward planning.

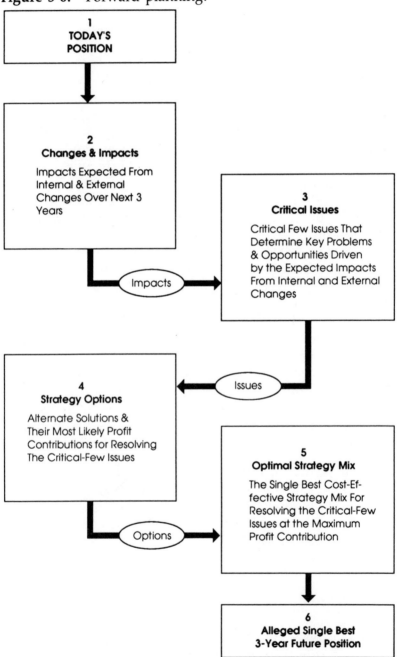

Figure 3-7. Backward planning.

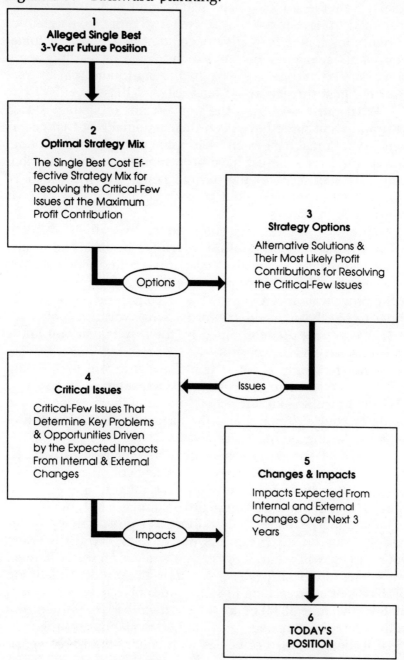

total of all the annual incremental contributions you must
have had to have made to a customer in order to maintain or
enhance his competitive advantage: to have kept the customer
"on plan." Year three becomes today. From its starting point,
you ask, "What must we have had to contribute year by year
over the past three years to have yielded these results?"

What must have been the smallest mix of strategies each
year and what must have been their minimal cost that got us
here? What must have been their optimal staging, scheduling,
and staffing? What must have been their individual contributions? By starting with the desired result you want to have
reached, you can make your plan account for it year by year
going back to the start.

With inward planning, your market drives the plan. With
backward planning, the future drives the decisions you must
make beforehand. Instead of year three being dependent on
achieving the objectives of year two, backward planning makes
it the other way around—year two becomes the result of year
three's objectives. In other words, what you must plan for
year two is now predetermined by the results that you know
you must achieve in year three.

Since hindsight is better than foresight, your backcasting
skills are better than forecasting. Backcasting gives you two
knowns to work from: the actual known of the present, which
becomes your end point; and the virtual known of the future
as your starting point.

Figure 3-8 shows the schematic representation of a backcast
plan for a petrochemical processor. A few critical assumptions
underlie its objectives: crude-oil cost ranges, a new plant
coming on stream, and competitive supplier shutdowns.

Planning retrospectively rather than prospectively forces
you to focus on the future of your business, which is when
your success will occur. It forces you to focus on the customers
who determine it. It protects you from the standard planning
problems of overreaching in setting your objectives, underesti-
mating the time it takes to realize them, or overstructuring
your strategies "just in case" rather than phasing them in
"just in time." It also coincides with your natural predisposi-
tions: It is easier to plan to get back to where you came from

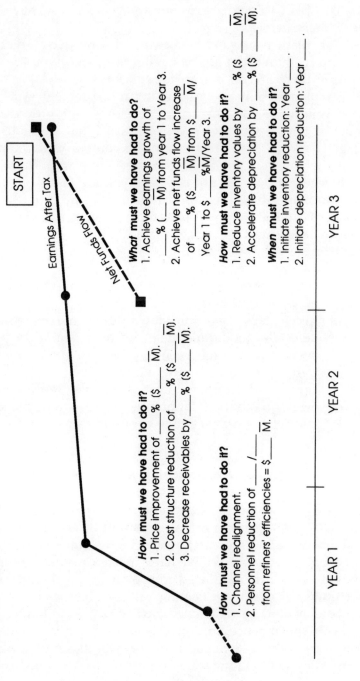

Figure 3-8. Backward plan.

START

Earnings After Tax

Net Funds Flow

What must we have had to do?
1. Achieve earnings growth of _____ % (_____ M) from year 1 to Year 3.
2. Achieve net funds flow increase of _____ % ($_____ M) from $_____ M/Year 1 to $_____ %M/Year 3.

How must we have had to do it?
1. Reduce inventory values by _____ % ($_____ M).
2. Accelerate depreciation by _____ % ($_____ M).

When must we have had to do it?
1. Initiate inventory reduction: Year _____
2. Initiate depreciation reduction: Year _____.

How must we have had to do it?
1. Price improvement of _____ % ($_____ M).
2. Cost structure reduction of _____ % ($_____ M).
3. Decrease receivables by _____ % ($_____ M).

How must we have had to do it?
1. Channel realignment.
2. Personnel reduction of _____/_____ from refiners' efficiencies = $_____ M.

YEAR 1   YEAR 2   YEAR 3

than to plan to get where you are going if you have never been there before.

No plan, backward or forward, is any good unless you stay on it. Either you are managing on plan or you are out of control; there are no points in between.

A plan is only as good as its measurement system. At each milestone you set up to measure your progress, you must be where you have planned to be. If not, you must plan to get back on plan. You cannot be content to say that you know where you are—that you are "off plan." There is no such place. If you are not on plan, you are lost.

No matter how meticulously you measure progress, your business can start to go off plan much sooner than you may be able to tell. There are three infallible early-warning signs of trouble:

1. Unit margins decline even though total profits on sales may continue to grow.
2. Receivables collection slows down due to returns of defective goods and disputes over quality or service even though total receivables may continue to grow.
3. Defections occur among major customers, major managers, and your high-producing sales representatives even though the total number of customers, managers, and representatives may continue to grow.

Taking Opportunities on the Rise

To manage a business "like you own it" is to be opportunistic. You seize opportunities or you go out of business. Your plans must be all about seizure: which opportunities, when they must be seized, and with what expected results. Dealing in brands exaggerates the need for opportunism. Brandable opportunities are fleet and fleeting. All their hair is in front; they are bald behind so that, once past, you can no longer grasp them. If you practice "undue diligence" by trying to learn all that is knowable before you take opportunities under management, they will no longer be opportunities. You must learn to be comfortable with an *owner's* sequence for hitting the mark:

1. Aim.
2. Fire.
3. Ready.

A few simple rules can help you and your management team aim quickly at apparent opportunities:

• Get enough understanding of an alleged opportunity to be able to rough out a position.
• Gain enough acceptance to get going. If you wait for consensus, you lose your chance.
• Assign individual roles and responsibilities. Publish clear standards, among which is a schedule of cut-off dates so you can control your risk. Offer compelling rewards.

Managing a branded business means managing the time value of money. Getting ready—really ready—takes time. Time costs cash flow. Today's dollar, today's market position, and today's satisfied customer are always worth more to you than the same dollar, market position, or satisfied customer tomorrow. Every dollar you earn today can be put to work today to turn it over into a greater value tomorrow. Opportunities that remain unseized incur a cost in tomorrow's values that can never be reclaimed. When you own a business, today is all you can ever own. Remember your Latin: *carpe diem* means "seize the day."

Many brandable opportunities, and the margins that go with taking them on the rise, never get any further than your fingertips. They are yours for the taking but you can never quite get your hands around them. Sometimes it is because you are myopic and cannot see them for what they are. At other times you may be greedy to keep all the goodies for yourself, or you may waffle about features and benefits, or you may leave the customer to last when he or she should be first. Once in a while, you may be all of the above, as were the anarchists of Xerox who developed the Star personal computer way out in front of the curve of the 1970s. They had no idea what to do with it. They thought they had to do everything themselves, leaving the customer as an afterthought. They never thought about the difference between a technology and a business. On the deathbed of their project, they left behind a four-point postmortem of how the Star fell through their hands:

• *Don't be myopic*. Pay attention to what other innovators are doing. In the 1970s, Xerox had its own powerful technical tradition that blinded Star's designers to the need to approach the market with cheap, stand-alone PCs. The result was a product that was highly unfamiliar to its customers' businesses.

• *Don't be greedy*. Be your industry standard, but make sure you create an industry whose standard you can be. Developing Star involved developing several enabling technologies. These technologies were unique in the industry. Xerox elected to keep them proprietary for fear of losing its competitive advantage. It would have been better to release them into the public domain or to market them early so that they could have become industry standards. Instead, alternative approaches developed at other companies became the industry standards.

• *Don't waffle about performance*. Set your specifications up front and lock them in. Star's designers should have established performance goals, documented them in the product's functional specifications, and stuck to them as they developed Star. When performance goals could not be met, the corresponding functionality should have been cut. For example, instead of going for speed, the designers could have made the user interface more responsive without necessarily executing functions faster.

• *Don't try to do everything yourself*. Bring the customer in. Star's designers tried to anticipate all of the applications that customers would want. Star should have been designed from the start to be open and extendable by users. The problem wasn't that Star lacked functionality. It was that it didn't have the functionality that customers wanted.

Even if you run an old, established business where you are top dog, taking opportunities on the rise is just as important to you as it is to a start-up manager. As far back as the mid-1980s, IBM had an opportunity to avert its restructuring of the mid-1990s. According to Chairman John Akers, "We asked ourselves, 'How well are we positioned?' Our market strength was in large hardware whereas market growth was taking place in software, services, and smaller machines. Furthermore, we were organized around hardware, not markets, and we weren't set up to solve customer problems."

Three years later, the opportunity was still there. By 1988, computer hardware accounted for a declining 57 percent of all customer spending on information processing. The other 43 percent went for software and related services, and it was still growing. One year later, the percentages reversed and the opportunity was lost. So were margins. From a 57 percent gross margin on sales in 1989, IBM dropped to a 40 percent margin in 1993.

Eternal vigilance is the price of margins. Markets change. Competition changes, both in form and substance. Technology changes. Even the rate of change of all these factors changes. Commoditization is the only constant—the direct result of parity competition, whose brand epitaph is "Turkey today, feather duster tomorrow." When a customer cries out, "What have you done for me lately?" he is inviting you to advantage him anew against the most recent inroad of commodity creep. By continually rebranding customer businesses, you can renew ownership of your margins.

4

Own Productivity

How Productivity Interacts With Applications and Margins

For want of productivity to generate a steady state of improved applications, the continuity of improving customer outcomes is lost.

For want of continuity of improved customer outcomes, branding as the industry standard is lost.

For want of branding, margins are lost.

If you are going to manage your business "like you own it," you must be the productivity king of your industry.

Nobody must be able to produce a more continuous supply of applications that can improve your customers' outcomes with equal or greater cost-effectiveness. You must be in the market every day, day after day, applying your improvements to customer operations. Day after day, you must be adding to your track record of reducing customer costs or expanding customer revenue streams. Any day you miss or any opportunity you miss out on to help a customer manage his assets better is a lost chance for you to improve your position as industry standard-bearer.

Productivity is the key to your ability to own a market. It gives you the gift of being able to work from a small asset base by turning it over in short cycle times. In doing so, you can be both a low-cost supplier and a fast time-to-marketer. If you use your time advantage to get to market first, the innovator's profits are available to you.

Managing productivity has five guidelines:

1. Keep your asset base small.
2. Automate everything that is cost-effective to automate.
3. Train your human assets to be the best.
4. Integrate your work flows.
5. Minimize your cycle times.

The five guidelines are all connected. Keeping small and being fast go hand in hand. So do keeping small and being well trained. So do being well trained and multiplying high performance through automation. Keeping small makes it easier to integrate your work flows, which adds quality to your productivity. Keeping small enables you to be a low-cost applier, which forms the baseline for high margins. Being fast helps you to be first.

Minimizing Your Asset Base

The basic formula for making the most money by managing "like you own it" is to maximize your return by maximizing your margins and minimizing the investment to achieve them. Your investment base becomes your asset base. You may call your assets by another name: facilities, capabilities, or resources. No matter what you call them, the family name of every asset is cost.

Taking ownership of a business means carrying its assets lock, stock, and barrel. Every day, your fixed assets must be paid for by your contribution margin. Your variable costs must be paid for by whatever is left over.

Asset bases are every manager's burden. You should approach the acquisition of any new asset warily, with knowledge beforehand of how much it will subtract from the profit contribution of your margins. Zero assets is a destination, not an objective. Nonetheless, you should make it your policy by interpreting it like this:

- Invest in only the assets you need to resource your core capabilities.
- Invest in them only when you need them, taking them on just in time rather than just in case.
- Reduce or divest every asset you do not need, do not need to own, or do not need to own outright.
- Before you acquire a new asset, ask yourself if you can lease it, rent it, share its ownership with a partner, or obtain it from an outsourcer.

Before empowerment made them owners, corporate managers were world-class asset collectors. They liked to build empires as long as someone else got the bill. Imperial asset bases turned out to be encumbrances. Trying to keep them strong everywhere ended up making them strong nowhere. Every attempt to keep them strong added another cost. As an owner manager, you cannot win points for your collection of assets. What you do with them is what counts: how much money you make for your customers and for your own business. This is what your productivity depends on.

When every dollar must earn its investment over and over again, make sure that your assets are concentrated on supporting your highest margin opportunities. Assets tied up in low-margin or no-margin businesses are like nonworking loans: your money goes out, but it does not come back with a profit.

No matter how carefully you manage, a growing business means asset trouble. Growth makes all businesses larger than they need to be, so that they are big beyond the focal length of their managers who are charged with maintaining the business vision. At two-thirds to one-half their size, these businesses could probably produce their same output at a fraction of the cost.

Ask yourself from time to time: "How big can we get before we become unproductive?" The answer may surprise you: not very big, and you start to become unproductive while you are a whole lot smaller than you think.

The smallest size business that maximizes your profits is the most productive. Productivity varies inversely with size.

So does innovation. The more people, the more committees, and the more management layers you impose between inventor and customer, the fewer innovations ever get to market first or at all. Instead of acting as merchants of innovation outcomes, your people become a perpetual debating society about what will work and what will not, what customers will buy and what they will not, and, most frustratingly, why change is unwise, unnecessary, or untimely.

Rightsizing as You Go

When you manage "like you own it," fixed assets are villains. Each represents a cost that your margins must pay for. Each requires management time and attention to keep it under control, accounting for more cost. You should require your assets to jump two hurdles:

1. How few do you need to realize your vision?
2. How few do you need to own?

Use Figure 4-1 as a model. Put your answers to the second question in the hub of the figure, under core capabilities. As you radiate outward from the hub, tag some of your noncore assets for spin-out as autonomous businesses that can outsource you and work with other companies as well. Tag others for leveraged buyouts, or see if you can cut their cost to you in half by joint-venturing them. If you can do none of the above with a noncore asset, pretty it up for divestiture.

Figure 4-1 provides a mechanism for rightsizing as you go. For every line of business that becomes a big winner and moves into your core as a strategic asset, move out a business at the low end. Turn it over while its value is still strong. Then go back and concentrate on your big winners. This is the way to continuously renew your business.

By rethinking your asset base and shrinking its fixed components, you can concentrate your funds where they will pay off. This is always where they can support your core

Figure 4-1. Downsizing your asset base.

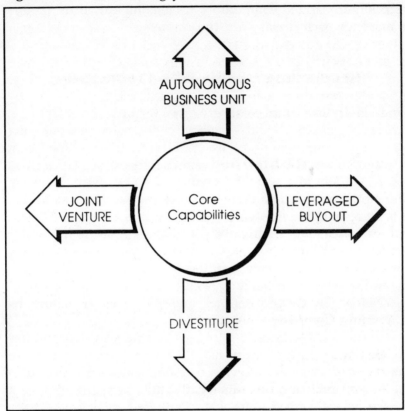

capabilities: as a marketer and merchandiser of improved customer outcomes.

Dell Computer is a case study in asset minimization. Dell competes against IBM, Digital Equipment, and Hewlett-Packard, all old-line, vertically integrated businesses. Michael Dell is a merchant. He owns no plants. Instead, he leases two small factories that assemble computers from outsourced parts. Dell's assembly operations are managed on a just-in-time basis, making a computer only after the order has been received. On an annualized basis, each dollar of Dell's fixed assets contributes thirty-five dollars to sales. At the same time, Dell's vertically integrated competitors are making only three dollars in sales for each dollar's worth of assets.

Reconciling Quality With Productivity

Productivity is resource-conservative. It minimizes asset use, especially people. Quality is resource-intensive, encouraging maximum employment of assets. Trying to combine them operationally is a business manager's version of "Eat all you want—yet still lose weight." Figure 4-2 shows why this is so: The more you focus on time-to-market productivity, the harder it is to approach zero-defect quality. The more emphasis you put on same-day shipments, the harder it is to minimize returns.

Your own best practice in the reconciliation of productivity and quality is probably bookended by two models, one of success by Southwest Airlines and the other of failure by Aluminum Company of America.

Southwest Airlines is a focused business. It concentrates on a market niche composed of business managers who require fast, frequent service on short-haul trips that take them out and back the same day. They want low cost and reliability; frills are dispensable. Southwest delivers a quality service in the form of successful flying outcomes by combining frequent schedules with few delays. To maximize productivity, the airline has standardized its assets on a single type of aircraft, the Boeing 737, to keep its labor, parts, and maintenance costs low. Downtime is minimized by easy access to parts inventories and by a labor force that requires training on only a single airplane model. Since no meals are served, turnaround time is kept to a minimum.

Southwest's asset utilization is maximized this way. So is the satisfaction of its customers, who have no plastic food or delayed flights to complain about.

ALCOA is another story. When the company split into autonomous business units, each manager was empowered to balance quality and productivity in his or her own way. The

Figure 4-2. Quality—productivity tradeoff.

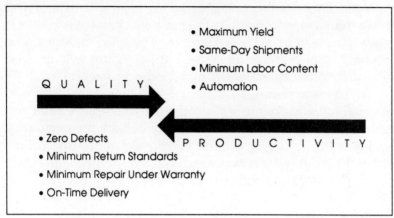

manager of the beverage-can sheetmetal business overcompensated on the side of productivity by reducing his head count 30 percent. By emphasizing shipments, he was able to achieve double-digit sales growth and raise one quarter's operating income by several million dollars. But quality caught up with him. Customer rejections and missed deliveries went up by an offsetting 25 percent.

If you want to operate as a best-of-breed business, your best practices must be in the operations that are critical success factors for your customers' outcomes. How good your best practices turn out to be depends on how well you manage their quality and productivity.

- Take manufacturing productivity. If you are best-of-breed, you may run out of materials four times a year. The median rate of your competitors may be as much as 400 times a year.
- Take delivery quality. If you are best-of-breed, you may ship late 2 percent of the time. The median rate of your competitors may be as much as 33 percent.

What if you only have one without the other: What good is productivity if it lacks quality?

As with all issues of managing a business "like you own it," reconciling your capabilities comes down to where you choose to invest your assets. On your own, you have to guess. Only your customers know for sure. They are the ones who are your ultimate reconcilers. Ask them. They will tell you how much better than your competitors you need to be at JIT (Just-In-Time) to reduce their rate of running out of materials. They will tell you how much better than your competitors you need to be at FTM (First To Market) to reduce their opportunity loss from unfillable orders. They will tell you the contributions these improvements need to make to their outcomes. In other words, they will set your objectives.

Marketcentering Your Productivity

Productivity is maximized when your customers are the beginning and end of all the work flows in your business: where everything you do is, from the first, customer-initiated, then customer-concurrent, and finally customer-satisfying. It is impossible to accomplish this operationally. You get maximum profit only if you organize for it.

If you run a one-market business, you can maximize your profit by organizing your business around it. This makes the architecture of your business and its work flows an *R&D extender* if you focus your applications on customer design and development processes; a *manufacturing extender* if you focus on customer manufacturing processes; or a *sales and marketing extender* if you focus on customer sales and marketing processes. In each case, your business is in the business of extending a customer's current capabilities so that they can add enhanced value to their outcomes.

Figure 4-3 shows a business that is centered on its market. The Residential Applications Marketcenter of a glassware manufacturer is segmented to serve two submarkets, one for exterior applications and the other for applications of glass technologies to residential interiors. Each capability of the Marketcenter is authorized by its correlate need in the market. The business is sized and structured to act as an

Figure 4-3. Residential applications marketcenter.

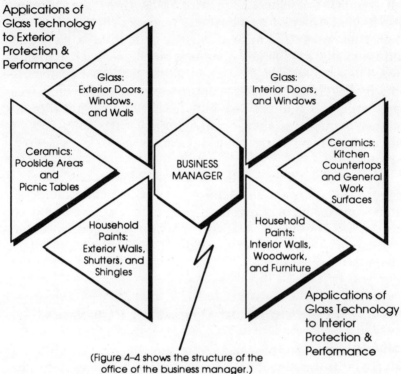

Applications of
Glass Technology
to Exterior
Protection &
Performance

Glass:
Exterior Doors,
Windows,
and Walls

Glass:
Interior Doors,
and Windows

Ceramics:
Poolside Areas
and
Picnic Tables

BUSINESS
MANAGER

Ceramics:
Kitchen
Countertops
and General
Work
Surfaces

Household
Paints:
Exterior Walls,
Shutters, and
Shingles

Household
Paints:
Interior Walls,
Woodwork,
and Furniture

Applications of
Glass Technology
to Interior
Protection &
Performance

(Figure 4–4 shows the structure of the
office of the business manager.)

outsourced skill base that picks up where its customers' skills leave off, acting as a supplementer and complementer of its customer businesses. It is also a source of some former customer capabilities that it can perform more cost-effectively.

By marketcentering your business on customer operating processes, you engineer them into your own operating processes structurally as well as conceptually. They are architected in, not just strategized in. From its skeleton on out, a marketcentered business is driven by the needs of your customer processes and not by your own processes, products, services, or systems. You do not have to remember to be customer-driven. You have no choice.

If you are a multimarket business, take the one-market

model and migrate it to each additional market. If you own a three-market business, organize it as three marketcenters. Each will be owned by a business manager chartered by his or her customers to improve their competitive advantage by adding value to their key operating outcomes. Each marketcentered business manager runs a profit-center whose customers— the managers of the operating processes he or she improves— are structurally integrated into his or her organization. An owner-manager is always managing in partnership *with* customer managers rather than developing *for* them or selling *to* them.

A model Office of the Business Manager is shown in Figure 4-4. Its structure equips you with your "cabinet" of four core resources: technical, materials, customer, and control. With this team, you can manage your marketcentered managers as their funder, consultant, and collector of internal revenues and profits.

Networking Your Operating Processes

The construction of your Office of the Business Manager shapes the organization of your core processes into three operating networks and a control function. This structure recognizes two rules of organization:

1. Its architecture must help ensure that you get the mix of quality and productivity that your customer outcomes demand.
2. Even when you think you have it down pat, you must encourage organization-model innovation as a continuous challenge to your people to reevaluate their business culture and the practices that no one wants to change because they are successful.

If there is such a thing as the ideal organization structure for you, it probably meets five criteria:

1. It consolidates a larger number of related functions into a smaller number of processes.

Figure 4-4. Office of the business manager.

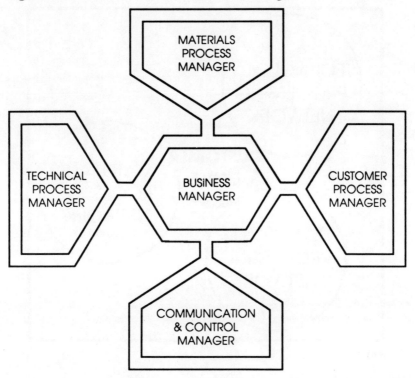

2. It consolidates a larger number of processes into a smaller number of networks.
3. It combines insourced and outsourced processes in each network.
4. It permits the work from each network's processes to flow cost-effectively into and out of its "supplier" and "customer" networks.
5. It positions customers as the drivers of each network's processes.

Figure 4-5 shows a market-centered organization model composed of three customer-driven networks that you can manage according to the strategies of owner-management.

• The model makes quality customer-originated, customer-defined, and customer-engineered since each core business is centered on its market. The business is organized as an autono-

Figure 4-5.   Marketcentered organization model.

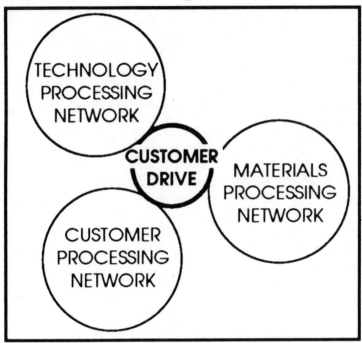

mous profit center that surrounds its customer niche, building customers structurally into its operations. Three criteria distinguish it:

1. Single market focus
2. Total customer dedication
3. Function-specific for each applications

• The model enhances productivity in two ways:

1. Interdependent operations are organized to work together within an integrated network. Each network is independent but interconnected with its partner networks. Their common driver is each customer marketcenter. Some operations in each network are core capa-

bilities; other functions can be outsourced, joint-ventured, or growth-partnered. Tying them together are information networks that incorporate their operations in real time no matter how far apart they may be or who owns them.
2. Marketcenter managers own the networks, not the other way around. As a result, managers can take their business elsewhere to get the best deal. This keeps network managers on their toes. Either they achieve continuous improvement or they become operationally obsolete as cost centers without redeeming value.

The progressive expansion of integrated information technology allows you to keep broadening your concept of what a business-function work team consists of. Online collaboration with "your people"—insourced and outsourced, local and global, core and peripheral—can be carried on instantaneously in real time and continuously across time zones all over the world, linking people according to what they do rather than where they are. In this way, your total work group never sleeps. Not a minute of continuous innovation needs to be lost.

Your ability to network everywhere can also bring your suppliers and customers into a work group's operations. If you are an apparel maker, for example, you can extend your network backward to worldwide textile suppliers and simultaneously forward to global retailers, bringing them together as well as with you at the same time any time.

Driving From Customer Outcomes

A verbal expansion of Figure 4-5 is shown in Figure 4-6, which takes each network apart to reveal the operating processes it incorporates and the functions that make up each process.

There are several things worth noting about each network:

1. The Technology Processing Network focuses on commercializing technology by making customers an integral part

Figure 4-6. Expanded marketcentered organization.

TECHNOLOGY PROCESSING NETWORK

1. Commercial Planning Process
   - Market Research Functions
   - Basic Research Functions
   - Product Development & Engineering Functions
2. Commercial Validation Process
   - Beta Testing Functions
   - Test Marketing Functions
3. Commercial Entry Process
   - Product Standardization Functions
   - Product Launch & Rollout Functions
   - Market Penetration Functions

MATERIALS PROCESSING NETWORK

1. Materials Acquisition Process
   - Forecasting Functions
   - Purchasing & Receiving Functions
   - Materials Inventory Functions
2. Materials Commercialization Process
   - Manufacturing Functions
     - Insourced
     - Outsourced

CUSTOMER PROCESSING NETWORK

1. Customer Generation Process
   - Finished-Goods Inventory Functions
   - Sales & Sales Support Functions
   - Order-Entry Functions
   - Credit Functions
2. Customer Satisfaction Process
   - Order Fulfillment Functions
   - Shipping & Delivery Functions
   - Installation & Maintenance Functions
   - Technical Support Functions
   - Outcome Value Assessment Functions
3. Customer Contribution Process
   - Pricing Functions
   - Billing & Collection Functions

of the innovative process from inception. Customers are present for commercial planning and play key roles in validating quality or productivity improvements that can come from applying a technology. In these ways, technology can be progressively tested for its contribution to customer outcomes before it goes to market at commercial entry.

2. The Materials Processing Network focuses on acquiring and commercializing the raw and finished materials that contribute to customer outcomes. The network's forecasting functions bring customers into materials processes from the start, giving market direction to the quality and productivity of manufacturing. For service businesses, the correlates of materials processing are data collection and decision support processes.

3. The Customer Processing Network focuses on generating and satisfying customers and collecting their high-margin contributions. It markets the applications flowing from the Technology and Materials Networks that have been market-tested and approved beforehand so that there are no surprises in their value-to-margin relationships. The productivity of customer processing is ensured as customers prevalidate the contributions they expect you to be able to make to their outcomes. Customer satisfaction with the quality of their outcomes is also ensured.

Each network's flow interfaces with the other two networks. Take the Technology Processing Network as an example:

- Commercial planning interfaces with customer generation in the Customer Processing Network. This allows customer inputs and sales information to be instilled into commercial planning for applications of technology as soon as they are conceptualized.
- Commercial validation interfaces with forecasting in the Materials Processing Network. This allows the results of beta testing and test marketing to be integrated into forecasts.
- Commercial entry interfaces with customer generation in

the Customer Processing Network. This allows product standardization to be integrated with finished-goods inventory. It also allows market-penetration planning to be linked up with sales.

The acid test of networking your process flows is found in two places: the *productivity* of your "deal flow," which is the number of closed deals you generate, and the "goodness" of each deal that reflects the *quality* of its outcomes.

Since productivity and quality are moving targets, your work flows are never networked once and for all. As with all forms of continuous improvement, they benefit best by a "rolling restructuring" that goes on a little each day. If you roll your restructuring, you should never need a major system reintegration or process reengineering. If you do, it is a sign of your failure to manage your business "like you own it."

Networking Your Strategic Alliances

Networking brings business and technology partners from inside and outside your operations into growth partnerships with you. It serves several purposes. It reduces the risk of going it alone. It reduces the assets you must buy and pay for to develop an application or enter a market with it. It reduces your time-to-market. It can also boost your productivity by giving you access to application-specific outsourcers.

Figure 4-7 shows your relationship with a networked supplier as mutual profit improvers. The figure also shows the profit-improving contribution that the two of you can make to a networked customer whose improved profits are shared with both of you in the form of high margins. The growth network operates like this:

1. Your supplier-partner contributes to your profits by reducing some of your critical costs and expanding some of your profitable revenue streams. These contributions grow your business. In return, you are able to reward your partner with high margins.
2. You and your supplier-partner contribute to a custom-

er's profits by reducing some of his critical costs and expanding some of his profitable revenue streams. In return, he rewards you with high margins.

A third cycle is implicit in growth networking, in which each of your customers contributes to the improvement of his own customers' profits. In return, his customers reward him with high margins. A portion of this reward is reinvested with you—and through you to your suppliers—to be recycled through the growth network.

A real-world example of growth networking is the interrelationship between IBM, Metaphor Computer Systems, and Procter & Gamble. In Figure 4-7, IBM is in the "you" position. P&G is a major customer for IBM to grow. Metaphor supplies IBM with a decision-support software program that runs on IBM computers. IBM sells an integrated system of hardware, software, training, and support to P&G brand managers to help them improve the contribution to their profits that can be made by improving the productivity of their promotion budgets. As promotion outcomes increase, so do P&G profits. As P&G profits increase, so do IBM margins. As IBM margins increase, so do Metaphor margins. Win-win becomes win-win-win.

Network growth is self-perpetuating. In effect, each network acts as a local-area growth market. Your supply partners serve as growth pumps for you. In turn, all of you serve as an integrated growth pump for a customer. The customer serves as a growth pump for his customers. Then the cash flows reverse. The customer's customers pump your customer's growth, which pumps your growth and your supplier-partners' growth. Reduced costs and expanded revenues flow one way. High margins flow the other way.

Passing Partners Through a Screen

Prospective supply partners should be screened with "the productivity question" first: How much value can we add together to my customers' outcomes over and above what I

Figure 4-7. Growth network.

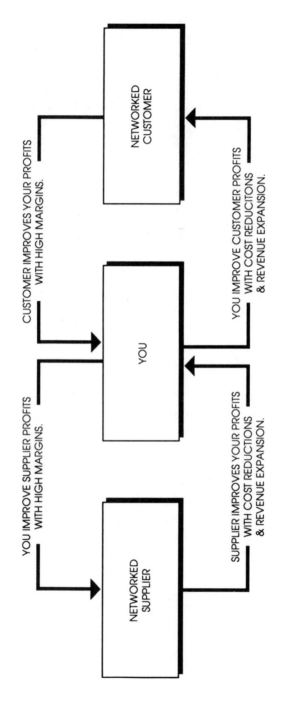

NETWORKED SUPPLIER

YOU

NETWORKED CUSTOMER

YOU IMPROVE SUPPLIER PROFITS WITH HIGH MARGINS.

SUPPLIER IMPROVES YOUR PROFITS WITH COST REDUCTIONS & REVENUE EXPANSION.

CUSTOMER IMPROVES YOUR PROFITS WITH HIGH MARGINS.

YOU IMPROVE CUSTOMER PROFITS WITH COST REDUCTIONS & REVENUE EXPANSION.

can add alone or with another partner? Your answer can have one or both of two parts:

1. We can add value by reducing even more the customer costs I am already helping to reduce, or by reducing other costs I am not currently able to reduce.

   - Which costs are reducible?
   - Are they on my customers' "must list" to reduce?
   - How much more can that add to my customers' outcomes?
   - How much more will that be worth to me after my partner has been compensated for his or her contribution?

2. We can add value by expanding even more the customer revenue streams I am already helping to expand or make more profitable, or by expanding other revenue streams I am not currently able to expand.

   - Which revenue streams are expandable?
   - Are they on my customers' "must list" to expand?
   - How much more can that add to my customers' outcomes?
   - How much more is that worth to me after my partner has been compensated for his or her contribution?

The added value of a partner has two components:

1. The difference between the total value the two of you can contribute to a customer's outcomes and the value that you can contribute alone.
2. The difference between the total value of the profits a partnership can contribute to you and the value of the profits that you can make alone.

At the same time that you are considering a prospective partner, he will be considering you. Both of you will be trying to calculate the same outcomes:

- Is the amount of proposed partnered growth significant enough for me to be interested?
- Is my own potential share significant enough for me to feel compelled to go ahead?
- Can I achieve similar growth by myself?
- Can I achieve similar growth faster with a different partner? Can I achieve it more surely? Can I achieve even greater growth with someone else?

A partnership's values are wholly opportunistic. They could not be achieved at all without the partnership. They reveal the opportunity cost of not partnering—the money that would otherwise be left on the table by both partners. Opportunistic or not, the values of partnering must be maximized.

Each prospective partner wants to know why he should not invest in his own business instead of with you. How do the returns compare? Which has quicker payback? Where is the lesser risk? You will want to know the same things.

Each prospective partner wants to know why he should not invest in another partner instead of with you. How do the returns compare? Which has quicker payback? Where is the lesser risk? You will want to know the same things.

You and each of your partners should have a good idea of where you want your partnerships to go before you sign on. You need to reach agreements such as these:

- Our business together will grow a minimum of 10 percent each year.
- Our business together will develop a minimum of $25 million in net sales with a minimum of $5 million in profits before taxes.
- Our business together will yield a minimum 30 percent pretax return on our combined investments.
- Our business together will realize a minimum of five times appreciation of capital over investment in its first 18 months.
- Our business together will achieve a minimum 40 percent gross margin on sales.

Two partnered objectives are more important than the rest:

1. Minimum acceptable return on investment (ROI) before taxes
2. Minimum annual net profit before taxes

In narrative form, a model statement of a growth partnership's objectives would say something like this: "The minimum objectives of the partnership are a pretax return on investment of 30 percent together with a $5 million cumulative net profit before taxes."

All other objectives, such as unit sales and their dollar volumes, rate of sales growth, percentage share of market, and total marketing investment, are supportive of ROI and profits.

Return on investment relates the partners' expected profits to the investments that they put at risk to earn them. The basic ROI formula defines profit as the rate of profit on sales or operating profit as a percentage of sales. Investment is defined as total capital assets employed to produce sales. As Figure 4-8 shows, ROI compares profit margin with asset turnover: a partnership's earnings in gross sales income related to the capital assets employed to generate them.

ROI is generally the best way to express the yield a partnership is getting out of its total capital employed, human and material. To manage ROI, you and your partners must know how to balance its two components.

One is profit margin expressed as the return on sales. It is affected by all the factors included in the total cost of sales: sales volume, price, product and service mix, and marketing and administrative expenses.

The second half of managing ROI is managing turnover of the investment base. It is affected by the movement of assets such as inventory, accounts receivable, and plant and equipment expenditures. A partnership's investment base is considered to be optimal when improvements in net profit are no longer possible by adding to or subtracting from its assets.

As a result of your mutual calculations, each of you must

Figure 4-8. Formulating partnership ROI.

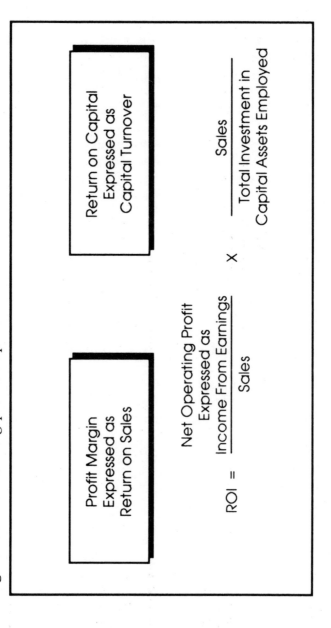

Profit Margin Expressed as Return on Sales

Return on Capital Expressed as Capital Turnover

$$ROI = \frac{Net\ Operating\ Profit\ Expressed\ as\ Income\ From\ Earnings}{Sales} \times \frac{Sales}{Total\ Investment\ in\ Capital\ Assets\ Employed}$$

be able to conclude that a dollar invested to be grown in a growth partnership is most likely to yield a more productive return than the same dollar invested in your own businesses or with another partner. In this way, you come into ownership—and coownership—of productivity.

Part Three
Managing Ownership

5

Own Management

When you manage a business "like you own it," there are three life-cycle events that tell you quickly and truly how good an owner you are.

The first comes at startup, when all you own is a "clean sheet of paper." What will you put on it that will make your fortune?

The second comes when you have to decide between vertical extension of your original business or horizontal diversification. Do you stay with the original definition of your game, or do you redefine it?

The third comes when you need to restructure, resize, or reengineer a mature business. What do you hold on to as your core?

The rest of the time, you will be getting by on your good looks and coming out clean on the thirty-day self-appraisal checklist shown in Figure 5-1.

Your self-appraisal gives you penultimate answers to how good an owner-manager you are—close to the ultimate, but not close enough to real ownership to be the acid test. What is your answer to the owner's ultimate question: "Could I go public?"

Could you take yourself and your team into the stock market and get funds? Would investors put their money on you to grow their assets?

Think of yourself making an initial public offering as an independent business. You must be able to look investors in the eye and say unequivocally: "*I am King of Outcomes* in my customer's industry. Buying into me is a blue-chip deal."

Whether your investors are your own top corporate man-

Figure 5-1.   Thirty-day self-appraisal checklist.

1. **Sales**
>Trace month-to-month performance.
>Compare each month this year to same month last year.
>Watch unit sales:
>>If they rise, is it from sales of more units or higher unit price?
>>If they fall, is loss of market share the cause?

2. **Costs**
>Watch out for month-to-month cost increases.
>Perform break-even analysis to reveal how much revenue the business
>needs to cover expenses and break even:

>Separate expenses into fixed and variable:

>>Fixed = Rent
>>Utilities
>>Management Pay
>>Constant Labor

>>Variable = Materials
>>Labor
>>Sales Commissions
>>Freight

>Track variable costs. Since they fluctuate with sales, calculate them
>not just in dollars but as a percentage of sales. This reveals incremental
>cost of incremental sales.

3. **Margins**
>Watch out for margin erosion.
>If margins decline, is it due to rise in expenses or to decrease in
>unit margins?

4. **Productivity**
>Watch payroll costs as a percentage of gross revenues.

5. **Turnover**
>Track month-to-month turn of inventory into receivables.

6. **Collections**
>Track month-to-month conversion of receivables into cash.

agers or outside stakeholders, they look for the same four clues to assess you as a manager of their assets:

- *How much* can I make on each dollar I invest?
- *How soon* before payback?
- *How long* will my investment continue to appreciate at growth rates?
- *How sure* can I be about "How much?" "How soon?" and "How long?"

In order to manage "like you own it," run your business from day one as if it were an independent public enterprise. Each business plan then acts as a "public offering"—a letter of agreement in which you contract to deliver specific income and outcome objectives to your corporate sources of funds in return for their money.

Under this scenario, you can come as close as possible to managing as an owner by restructuring the vision of your business from a corporate strategic business unit to a *virtual business*. A virtual business is an almost-but-not-quite autonomous company: virtually but not actually a stand-alone, independent entity that owns the application skills, the margin capability, and the operating productivity to grow *its* outcomes by growing the outcomes of its customers. With this vision as your guidance, you will be able to take on the look and feel—and preoccupations—of an entrepreneurial owner-manager:

1. *Is my return on market position high enough?* Am I minimizing my cost base and making sure that the incremental profits from maximizing my market position exceed their incremental costs?
2. *Are my outcomes proprietary enough?* Am I capturing the most significant outcomes so I can be their standard-bearer, and are my outcomes meaningfully differentiated from competition?
3. *Is my strategy mix optimal?* Am I concentrating my resources into a minimal mix of the fewest best strategies? Are they driven by my customers' outcomes? Are

they pointed at solving customer needs rather than memorializing my technologies?

4. *Is my control system tight enough?* Am I front-end loading my measuring and monitoring benchmarks so that I have early warnings on defaults and I can evaluate performance-to-date in advance of each major commitment of new resources?

5. *Is my eye on what comes next?* Am I running the business at least 20 percent for tomorrow? Will tomorrow be ready for me when I come to it?

There is one more area of expertise in which you must hold the industry standard. If you want to be king of the appliers, you must be king of the measurement of your outcomes. *In order to own the standard, you must own its measurement.* A measurement system that you and your customers can jointly trust to assess your continuous improvement of their operations is indispensable to agreement with them on quantifying your values so you can base your margins on them. There are two values you must be able to assess for each outcome: the dollar value of *how much* improvement you add on a before-and-after basis, and the time value of *how soon* you are able to add it after a customer gives you the go-ahead.

If things ever start to go bad for you, the first place to look is at yourself. Bad management or mistakes in managing your business are most likely to come from five sources:

1. You have overexpanded or tried to expand too fast.
2. You have let your costs get out of hand by letting inefficiencies creep into major operations.
3. You are paying too much for innovation beyond the point of "good enough."
4. Your applications mix is out of sync with demand, or you have allowed it to become top-heavy with low-margin applications.
5. You have failed to anticipate a changed environment.

In your markets, your business depends for its position on the economic value added (EVA) to your customers. The economic-value standard works the same way internally. Your profitability depends on the EVA contributed by each operation. Since EVA is calculated as after-tax operating profit minus the total annual cost of capital, it makes it necessary for you to know what your capital is costing you and whether or not you are beating its cost with the earnings it contributes. Unless your returns exceed your cost of capital, you are in trouble. Only when you are consistently beating your capital costs—not just making positive operating earnings—can you claim to be on top of your business.

Three strategies will help you manage your EVA:

1. Earn more profit on your existing capital by being more productive or cutting costs or both.
2. Employ less capital to keep profits the same.
3. Invest capital in high-return projects that can earn more than the total cost of the capital employed.

Managing a People-Dependent Business

Managing is people-dependent. No matter how intelligent your products, services, or systems are, they do not apply themselves. Applications is people-intensive and, in terms of its requisite skillsets, people-specific. Good appliers may be born, not made. But they can be made better. The good ones are hands-on people. They love to get their hands on a customer's operation. They know where to put their hands because they know the operation. They know the operation because they come from it, having worked in it as insiders before coming back to it from the outside.

If the operation is a cost-centered business function such as nonferrous manufacturing, good appliers know where its costs are. They know how much the costs normally amount to. They know how those costs differ from a ferrous-manufacturer's costs. When they find costs that are excessive, they know how to bring them back in line.

If a customer's operation is a profit-centered line of business such as computer work stations, good appliers know

how it makes money. They know what its distribution channels are, who composes its market, and what its margins
should be. When they find margins that are below average,
they know how to bring them back in line.

Good appliers follow a process. They use their diagnostic
skills to compare a customer's outcomes with their norms.
This enables them to measure the "goodness" or "badness" of
an operation. They use their prescriptive skills to specify the
single best application to improve the operation's outcome: to
cut back on the badness and step up the goodness. They use
their project management skills to partner with the customer's
people to co-manage the improvement and "get to outcome"
fast.

A good applier can walk into an automobile manufacturer's
plant and ask the "critical few" questions that are the basis for
his or her diagnosis. How long is it taking you to design,
develop, and deliver a new model? If it is taking you more
than 46 months from start to finish, we need to talk. How
many engineering hours are involved? If it is taking you more
than 1.7 million hours, we need to talk about that, too. How
many hours does it take you to produce each car? If it is taking
you more than 16.8 hours, we can include that in our discus-
sions. These numbers are my customers' norms—the cumula-
tive average of the outcomes they normally achieve as a result
of our work together. What if I can help you come closer to
them? How much will that contribute to your competitive
advantage?

If it takes a customer 60 months from design to delivery
and an average of 3 million engineering hours, and if it takes
from 25.1 to 36.2 hours to produce each car, a good applier
knows the added value of each month and each hour he or
she can save from the customer's current outcomes. The good
applier also knows how much it will be worth to the customer
to install the improvements. This, not a price book, sets the
practitioner's fee.

Appliers work best in small, focused teams, zeroed in on
a single business function or line of business in a single
customer industry. When major functions are similar—as they
are between food or drug processing and chemicals process-

ing—or when different business lines have similar markets and distribution channels—like consumer packaged goods and financial services, both of which are sold through retailing "supermarkets"—an applications team may be bifocal:

- An applications team whose mission is to be a cost controller of customer operating assets in a business function must know all there is to know about how to reduce the costs contributed by the function's work flows and cycle times.
- An applications team whose mission is to be a sales developer of customer products and services in a line of business must know all there is to know about how to increase the revenues and earnings contributed by the business line's sales and marketing work flows and sales cycle times.

At General Motors, the new team approach is focused on producing "more and better cars with fewer people." Don Runkle, vice president of advanced engineering, remembers how it was before teaming, when everything at GM used to be departmentalized by function: "I hate to admit it, but we might have designed a car three times before getting it right."

ALCOA has set up a new-wave business team in a trailer to manage applications of an innovative aluminum-and-fiber sheet metal. To keep costs down and people together, ALCOA's team eats its power lunches at a local "Eat 'N' Park." They show their team spirit by referring to themselves as "The Oakland Raiders of ALCOA."

ALCOA's Raiders set "manage like you own it" ground rules for themselves:

- Autonomy
- Separate identity and facilities
- Narrow focus
- Total dedication on sink-or-swim basis
- Minimal funding without hope of more
- Lots of latitude
- Ownership stake

Working cheek-by-jowl in a trailer, ALCOA's team members are able to communicate quickly and directly. They work without going through intermediaries, writing memos, or leaving voicemail. They make it impossible for meddlers to work themselves in edgewise. Ford's Taurus team, which has the same mindset, has a similar commitment to easy communication. "What the customer wants is the first order of business, followed by what is feasible financially, and how a new design can be manufactured most efficiently by factory workers." These things are all that the team talks about. They talk about them all the time.

Other car companies and manufacturing businesses are using independent product "platform teams" to move ownership all the way down in their organizations to the point where it comes closest to the customer. Each platform team is multidisciplined. It combines engineers, designers, and product experts who work together with financial, sales, and marketing people and, in many cases, with their future customers. In effect, each team is a minibusiness.

In addition to enabling people to talk to each other, organizing your people into applications "leanteams" can give you four more advantages:

1. When decisions have to be made, everybody on the team is there to contribute to them.
2. Everybody can wear more than one hat because everybody on the team knows enough about everybody else's job to step in and do it in a pinch. Once your people become multifunctional, you can mix and match them in the ideal configuration for each project.
3. Everybody on the team knows how the business is doing and what he or she must do to make it better.
4. Nobody feels that everything depends on him or her. But everybody on the team knows that everybody else is depending on him or her to get the job done.

The only way to ensure that you get your full share of these advantages is to keep the number of management levels your teams report to down to one: yourself. The downside of eliminating middlemen is that you increase your span of control. But on the upside, you keep your organization chart simple, your authority remains undiluted, and you are always in control of your business.

Modeling an Applications Team

The minimal applications team contains three resources:

1. A technical-process resource
2. A materials-process resource
3. A customer-process resource

A model team composed of these core capabilities is shown in Figure 5-2. It is a line version of the Office of the Business Manager team shown in Figure 4-4. Supplemental capabilities can be insourced and outsourced on an ad hoc basis as required.

A team manager meets your standards of performance when he or she operates the team so that:

- According to its plan, stretch profit objectives are set and met—first for the customer and then for the team—so that a true partnership in profit improvement is created.
- Strategies are maintained as a minimal mix, with the team applying only the smallest number of strategies to each project that ensure maximum improvement of customer profits.
- The team's product or service applications command a premium price because they are differentiated from competition by the amount, rate, and dependability of their contribution to profitable customer outcomes.
- As a result, the amount of customer profits that the team's applications are able to supply becomes the standard of value for its industry.
- The team is the leading profit maker in its industry and maintains that position by achieving an annually increasing rate of earnings growth.

Figure 5-2. Model applications team.

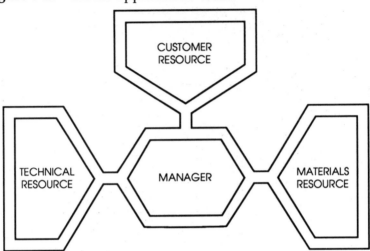

- Team productivity is measured by the value of customer assets under management per team member.

As you manage your team-based organization structure, get into the habit of asking yourself a short list of questions:

- *Capacity utilization.* Is each team member being utilized to the full extent of his or her capacity? Can fuller utilization be achieved by improved teaming or a realignment of how tasks are sequenced?
- *Work flow.* Is the flow of work from one team member to the next the shortest distance between two points? Can faster flow and shorter cycle times be achieved by making tasks smaller and simpler or by distributing tasks that are centralized?
- *Work clusters.* Is related work clustered together into small subgroups composed of team members who contribute to the same work flows? Are team members spending almost their total work time together?

There is a point at which the team concept becomes self-limiting. Owner-managers and their people should think of themselves as microcompanies, each with its own "company" name that relates it to its market, and a business case and mission that reflect its customers' compelling need to do business with it: in other words, the market's reason for its existence. The team spirit required for diverse disciplines to pull together comes best from an entrepreneurial "us against the world" commitment. The accompanying contempt for failure must be inbred. The only acceptable answer for you and each member of your business to the question: "What will you do if you don't make plan?" is "Make plan."

For both yourself and your team, you must be failure-intolerant. As a manager, you get the failure rate you tolerate. If you permit yourself and your key players to make mistakes, or, even worse, if you tell them that not making mistakes proves that they are not trying hard enough or innovating boldly enough, your reward will be mistakes. By making failures acceptable, you reinforce the propensity of your people to make them. The more they make, the better they become at making them. Like success, failure is a learned response. Each forgiven failure breeds the next one. Through repetition, one-time losers become proficient in losing.

Forgiveness for failure to improve customer outcomes is misplaced altruism. It substitutes your personal judgment of what is satisfactory for the professional judgment imposed by customer satisfaction. As your customers are sure to let you know, it is not satisfactory for them to miss out on an opportunity to improve one of their outcomes because of you. Nor is it satisfactory for them to hear you say you are sorry and offer to refund their money or make it up to them the next time. The opportunity cost they suffer from missing out on realizing the time value of their money can never be made up.

The magic of teams is that their members can be bonded into a unit that they will live and die for, yet they can still show their individual creativity. Only a few need to take full advantage of the opportunity to stand out for a team to be unusually successful. As on a National Hockey League squad

of twenty-five, only three to five players need to be great for
the team to win big.

Modeling an Owner's Management Style

When you manage a business composed of autonomous applications teams, style is crucial. The National Football League
will provide you with a model. Each year its teams draft from
the same labor pool of college players. Since the last-place
team chooses first, variations in talent level off over time. Yet
in over twenty-five years, before established players won the
right to market themselves as free agents, nine teams had
never once played in the Super Bowl. These are all teams that
made repeated mistakes in choosing coaches. They have found
that mistakes at the top take a long time to discover and even
longer to correct, which has made them difficult to recover
from. They have left behind a long-term legacy of faulty
leadership that has failed to recognize the capabilities of even
superior talent, or to apply it.

In managing "like you own it," there is no substitute for a
powerful chief. That means three things: managing your people directively, managing them by standards of high performance, and managing a high-reward system to compensate
them for high achievement.

1. *Manage directively.* Owner-managers manage personally, subjectively, and directively. In making policy, they invite
consultation but shun consensus. Once policy is agreed on,
commitment must follow the way the manager calls the shots.
Since the buck stops with you, all prerogatives begin with
you. In this way, you steer and each team rows. If everyone on
the team steers—which is what happens under consensus—no
one rows. You go nowhere.

2. *Manage by standards of high performance.* Small, autonomous work teams of highly self-motivated people are the high
achievers in every business. Anyone who needs to be moti-
vated is a wrong player. For the right players, the chance to
achieve a high reward in a higher-than-average-risk situation

is its own motivation. That is how you can tell who the right players are: They come with high performance standards as their natural norms. Each player's VAP score—the value added by each player—is high. As a result, so is the value added by each value-adding team [VAT].

3. *Manage a high-reward system.* High shared rewards are the payoff for high shared performance. You should reward your people for three things:

a. Individual performance, to encourage initiative
b. Team performance, to encourage partnering
c. Individual skill development, to encourage the acquisition of multiple competencies so that each individual can be a versatile team player

Paying and Being Paid for Performance

If you are going to manage your business "like you own it," you should own a stake in it. So should your key players. Your compensation package as well as theirs should be made up of three value-creating components:

1. Stock options: shares of corporate stock valued at a percentage—10 percent is a norm—of each year's compensation, in the manner of Pepsico, Merck, Warner-Lambert, Nynex, and Du Pont middle managers.
2. Phantom stock: virtual shares that grow in value in proportion to the growth in the value of your business and that are convertible into cash awards.
3. Performance payments: cash bonuses for a weighted mix of
   • Achievement of key milestone events in the growth of your business "on plan" or ahead of plan
   • Improvement in customer profits

To provide the proper incentive, bonuses should have a pay-for-performance ratio of bonus to salary of around 3:1.

That sets up the carrot for smart, hard work. Stock options should also encourage stretch performance. If you price them at a 25 percent premium over their market price on the day you make each grant, your managers must jump the hurdle rate for stockholders before they can exercise their own options.

This compensation model highlights the three things you get paid for as an owner-manager. One, you get paid for long-term value creation for your own business and for the customers that you are in business to grow. Two, you get paid for your future performance, not your past experience. Three, you get paid for making a high-performance business plan and for staying on top of it.

A combined stock-and-performance payment compensation plan gives you three benefits:

1. You and your people buy into "ownership."
2. Your rewards are tied to value creation. This enables you to control them. It also puts no topside cap on their total amount.
3. You and your key players can be rewarded individually and as a team. This type of incentive-leveraged package, on top of regular salary and benefits, allows salary to be the lowest component of the plan. This helps to keep fixed costs low.

The heart of all high-performance reward systems is pay for performance. Performance pay drives progress by recognizing it. The size of each payment should reflect the size of the achievement and the degree of difficulty that has to be overcome. A whole menu of critical success events can be recognized:

- Entering a market on time or earlier
- Staying within budget or achieving a budget surplus
- Optimizing product quality, with attendant freedom from repairs under warranty, replacements, or recalls
- Maintaining uptime
- Maximizing productivity and balancing it with optimal quality
- Minimizing time-to-market

- Maximizing accounts receivable collections
- Maximizing same-day order fulfillment
- Maintaining zero-based inventory
- Maintaining continuous innovation regime
- Maintaining margins
- Winning major sales
- Minimizing fixed costs
- Optimizing customer satisfaction

Each event is cause for rejoicing. But it must always be tempered with a cautionary note that says, "Congratulations. You're vulnerable." What you are vulnerable to is downside shock. Upside rewards should be counterbalanced by penalties if performance milestones go unmet or are not met on time. When your people make plan, they should benefit. When they go off plan, they should pay for it with a subtraction from their benefits. This point-and-counterpoint of deposits and withdrawals is the way of the real world.

Nobody plays to win in business for money alone. But nobody plays to win without it. For owner-managers and their teams, the sharing mix needs to be revised. The old 80–20 allocation of rewards, in which top management keeps the eighty, must be upended. The businesses must get the eighty. Corporate management must earn its twenty for consultation, bankrolling, and support services. Corporate management is a crafter of business teams, not a player; a dealer in capabilities and opportunities, not a dealmaker. That needs to be rewarded, but at the 20 percent level.

By the year 2000, most medium-size minicorps and all the largest megacorps will be virtual corporations. Their sources of income will be self-managing organizations that own their businesses. All the traditional corporate functions will be attached to their businesses or will be autonomous businesses themselves. But they will have to do a lot better than the thirty-eight business teams comprising 1,400 workers at the Bausch & Lomb eye care products plant near Rochester, New York. The teams were set up in 1989 when twenty supervisors were taught team leadership and told to manage "like they own it." As late as 1993, nothing had happened.

Along with everybody else, Bausch & Lomb has begun to

learn that the mere act of giving twenty managers the power to put together thirty-eight multidisciplined teams and develop products or services into businesses accomplishes exactly nothing unless the managers know *how* to do it and their teams know *how much* they stand to benefit.

Not all twenty empowered managers are able to do it even if they know how. Not all 1,400 members of thirty-eight empowered businesses are able to do it even when they know how much it can benefit them. More fail than succeed. For them, old habits prove stronger than new power; tradition proves more powerful than change; averting risk is more attractive than the allure of unlimited reward.

For you, this can be your opportunity to own it.

Index

absolute profitability, 76
accounts receivable, 65
  turnover, 65
  turnover ratio, 71
activity ratios, 71
added value, 63, 108, 129
  net, 31
Advanced Micro Devices, 1
Aetna Life & Casualty
  Insurance, 8
Akers, John, 89
ALCOA, 7–8, 96–97
  teams, 123–124
Allis-Chalmers, 10
Apollo, 18
applications, 37–60
  brands, 53–59
  continuous improvement,
    51
  converting technology to,
    42–46
  "good enoughness,"
    48–51
  home for, 38
  innovator's edge, 46–48
  marketable values, 39
  opportunities, 39–42

  optimizing customer asset
    management, 59–60
  value-based pricing and,
    74
applications kingdom, 4
asset base, 23
  downsizing, 95
  minimizing, 92–94
  turnover, 91, 111
  visualizing, 27–30
assets, 2, 13
  benefit values, 40
  risk of mismanaging, 9
autonomous business, from
    noncore assets, 94

backcasting, 80, 84
backward planning, 83, 85
Bausch & Lomb, 131
Bethlehem Steel, 10
B. F. Goodrich, 9
brands, 53–59
  definition, 12
  distribution, 57–58
  margins to indicate, 61
  opportunities for, 86–87
break-even